A Genealogy of John Gosbee, the Brewer

Compiled by
Patricia Lumsden

May, 2011

ISBN 978-0-557-73147-3

Genealogy

Doing genealogy is not a cold gathering of facts but, instead, breathing life into all who have gone before.

We do not judge the ancestors as we did not walk in their shoes.

It goes beyond just documenting facts. It goes to pride in what the ancestors were able to accomplish, how they contributed to what we are today. It goes to respecting their hardships and losses, their never giving in or giving up, their resoluteness to go on and build a life for their family.

That is why I do genealogy, and that is what calls those young and old to step up and restore the memory or greet those whom we had never known before.

~

Genealogy is my hobby; I have been researching various families for more than 30 years. I gathered most of the information contained in this brook from published sources, official records and documents and from information given to me by others researching the same lines, or freely sharing what they know. My goal is to make this information available to anyone who wants it. If any errors or omissions are found, please be kind and let me know.

Patricia Lumsden
patricial_@hotmail.com

The Name Gosby

This is an English locational surname, but of Danish-Viking pre 7th century origins. It originates either from the village of Girsby in the county of Lincolnshire, or possibly from a now "lost" medieval village of which the only memory today is the surname.

This is recorded in several spellings including Gisby, Gisbye, Guisby and the rare Gosby, although there may be other forms that have not been iddentified.

The village of Girsby has itself undergone many spelling changes in the thousand years or so since it was first recorded. These include Grisberi in the Anglo-Saxon Chronicles of the year 1050, and again in the famous 1086 Domesday Book of William 1st, and later still as Grisbi.

The name probably means either the farm "bi", belonging to "a youth" from the Olde English "gurle", or it may have been the Viking personal name "Griss" meaning grey, as in grey haired.

Locational surnames of this type usually developed after the villagers left the village and moved elsewhere in search of work. When this happened they often took, or were given, as their surname, the name of their original village. We do know in this case that the name was well recorded in London from the late 16th century.

Examples of the recordings taken from these early church registers include Michael Gisby, a witness at the famous church of St Dunstans in the East, Stepney, on June 22nd 1606, and Jone Gisbye, married at St Mary Whitechapel, London, on June 12th 1671. The earliest recording may be that of Joan Gysebye, who married William Page, at St Brides church, Fleet Street, London, on Oct. 28th 1594. [Ref 001]

~ John Gosbee ~

The first to bring the Gosbee line to Canada was John Gosbee, of Canturbury, Kent, England. There are many records of Gosbees in the Canturbury area.

1.) **John** Gosby (Gosbee) was born in England @1710. He married Mary Rogers on June 24/1731 at St. George the Martyr Church, Canterbury, Kent, England. **Children:**
1.1) John Gosby, who was christened on Sept. 26/1731 (same church as above). There is no further information on this son, so it is assumed that the child died prior to the family's emigration to Nova Scotia.
1.2) Jane Gosby who was born in 1748, in London, England.

John and Mary Gosby emigrated to Nova Scotia. They arrived in Halifax on the ship ***ALEXANDER*** in 1749. He is shown as being a husbandman (farmer), married to Mary, with one girl and one female servant. Soon after their arrival in the new town of Halifax, another **son:**
1.3) Lewis Magee Gosbee was born. He was baptised at St. Paul's Church on July 23/1749.

Tragedy stuck the family soon after, when John and Mary's baby daughter, Jane, died in December. She was buried on Dec. 28/1749. Shortly before his second birthday, Lewis Magee Gosbee died. He was buried on June 13/1751.

A fourth **child**, a daughter:
1.4) Sarah Gosbee was born in 1751, and baptised on Nov. 21 of that year. She was the first child to survive to maturity. She married Seth Webb. [Ref. 1.4] She was mentioned in her father's will as Sarah Webb.

John's wife, Mary Gosbee, died in 1755, and is buried in St. Paul's Cemetery, Halifax. John Gosbee remarried on Nov. 21/1763. His new wife was Elizabeth Laurilliard, the daughter of Jean-Christophe (Jonathan Christopher) and Anne

(Clement) Laurilliard. ***(See back pages for genealogy of the Laurilliard family.)***

John and Elizabeth Gosbee had five more **children:**
1.5) William Gosbee was the first child born. His life was short; he died on January 31/1765.

1.6) Susannah Gosbee was baptised on December 1/1765 at St. Pauls' Church, Halifax. Susannah survived to maturity and married Matthew Walker in 1791. They had a large family. Matthew was a carpenter. A son, Matthew Walker (b: 1796) married Mary Jane Laurilliard.

1.7) Charles Gosbee was baptised on July 23/1767. He died on Sept. 17/1772. A photo of his headstone appears in ***Morse's Gravestones***.

1.8) A daughter, Elizabeth Gosbee was born in Dec., 1769. She died at 11 months of age, on Nov. 3/1770.

1.9) John Gosbee was the only son to survive to maturity. A birthdate has not been found yet, but he is mentioned in his father's will. Most, if not all, of the Gosbee families of Nova Scotia and Prince Edward Island descend from this son, John Gosbee. His descendants are also spread over many of the United States. The name is also spelled Gosby, Gosbey, Gosbie.

Although John Gosbee (1st) was listed as a husbandman, or farmer, at the time of his arrival in Halifax in 1749, there is little doubt that he was, instead, a brewer. The offer to qualified English subjects (farmers, carpenters, etc.) was tempting to the overcrowded masses of London - fifty acres of land plus ten for every member of his family, together with arms, ammunition and "a proper quantity of materials and utensils for husbandry, clearing and cultivating the lands, erecting habitations, carrying on the fishery, and such other purposes as shall be deemed necessary for their support."

"The people who...registered were largely the poor of London...cockneys wholly unfit for a life in the...wilderness." "One may wonder how reliable were the statements of occupations entered into the passenger lists...the numbers who put themselves down as "husbandmen" "carpenters", "joiners", etc. look suspiciously large". Regardless of their prior occupations, hundreds of families were accepted as settlers for the new town and they set sail in the spring of 1749. (Ref 004)

The Halifax in the very early years of settlement was raw. Taverns were on every corner and lawnessness was rife. In order to cut down the number of drinking establishments in the town, the Council of Halifax resolved to limit the number of liquor licenses to 40. As an inducement to brewers of the town, land grants were offered in the Windsor area, and all along the Windsor - Halifax road.

John Gosbee's name is found among those who were granted land in the Windsor area, and for a number of years he lived in that area, owning large tracts of land and several town lots as well. His name appears on the Crown grant of Newport Township in July 1761, as a person applying for liquor licenses.

Prior to his marriage to Elizabeth Laurilliard, John Gosbee owned the following lots of land:

- D - in 1st Division #1 Town of Newport
- 1 - 6 acre lot: B - 4th Division #8
- 1 - farm lot or tract: E - 2nd Division #2 - 200 acres
- Village lot so called B:2nd Division # 3 included as part of the farm lot
- 1 - lot in the Grand dyke near the Town Plot B:3rd division # 5 - 10 acres
- 1 - lot Marsh land in the Commonage A:3rd Division # 1
- 1 - out lot Kennetcook, Township of Newport being woodland approximately 125 acres.
- 1 - other lot of wild or woodland being near part of the Road leading to Halifax and within the limits of the

township of Newport approx. 425 acres.

A land grant petition in 1770 by John Gosbee, John and George Laurilliard, asked for 1500 acres (500 each) at the Northwest Arm, Halifax. A note by C. Morris, Surveyor, states: "Gosbee got his grant, but the others, John and George Laurell (sic) refused their grant."

It's not known exactly when John and family moved back to Halifax, or whether he did take up residence on the above mentioned property, but it is known that he did have brew shops on Argyle Street and Grafton Street in Halifax. During his lifetime, John Gosbee accumulated much property and other assets.

The Nova Scotia newspaper of the day – The Gazette – offered advertising columns, and John Gosbee, on Grafton Street, advertised his brewery in 1772. [Ref 002]

John's death occurred in 1777. His wife, Elizabeth was the executrix and his brother-in-law, George Laurilliard was one of the bondsmen. His will is dated April 7/1777. He left to his "Daughter Sarrah Webb" one shilling, the rest to his wife Elizabeth Gosbee for the care of his two "infant" (under the legal age) children, John and Susanna.

The settlement of his estate involved selling off much of his assets, although his family retained a house and lot in Halifax. Some of the assets that were sold at public auction included: "Brew House, stable, Utensils and the lotts of Land Inclosed with a fence about it". Letter E, # 6 and 7 and part of #8. ¾ of E # 15 Grafton Street, all in Ewers Division with brew house on said premises and fixtures, vats, etc. sold to John Osterman for 185 lbs.

1 lot Letter C # 1 Callanders division with Dwelling house. 2 lots Letter A # 9 and 10 Ewers Division. 1 lot Letter J # 6. Sold to John Osterman, Brewer for 76 lbs. 10 shillings. The following items were auctioned individually - *(Pounds: Shillings: Pence)*:

- One Feather Bed 3:3:0

- One Pair of Candlesticks 0:6:6
- One Pair of Flat Irons 0:6:10
- 1 Toasting Iron 0:1:6
- One Copper Saucepan 0:2:0

The following were auctioned at a total value of 3:0:0.

- 1 Coat and Waistcoat
- 5 Coarse shirts
- 1 Old great Coat
- 1 Old Goun
- 1 Hat
- 1 Old Pair of Shoes

Land: Lot #1 - Goodwood Division, Halifax. 500 acres, to Jeremiah Marshman for 40 lbs.

Elizabeth Gosbee sold off other land in the years to come. Several other transactions are recorded. In 1782 she sold a lot on Grafton Street, Letter E #1 Ewers Division, with dwelling house and all other buildings, to Richard Kidston for 100 lbs.

There is record of a court case involving Elizabeth and her brother, George Laurilliard, Shipwright, in December, 1777. It is not clear whether this is involved with the settlement of John Gosbee's estate. Perhaps George Laurilliard owed money to John (on Sept. 20/1773, John Gosbee sold a lot of land and a house on Grafton Street, Halifax to him) and this was a necessary action to settle the estate? The date is so close to that of John's death in 1777. Regardless, Elizabeth won the case, receiving 20 lbs., damages worth 35 lbs, a House in Grafton Street was attached "***known by the Sign of the Bacchus***". Elizabeth was referred to as a "mantua maker". (Ref. 005) She no doubt learned this trade from her father, Jean-Christophe Laurilliard, who was a tailor, as were other of his descendants. Elizabeth died in December, 1799.

~ Further Generations ~
1.9) John Gosbee and his Descendants

1.9) John Gosbee was a Shipwright[(Ref. 1.9a)]. He had his shipbuilding operations in the "north suburbs" of Halifax, prior to his move to the Country Harbour area of Guysborough County. The lot in Halifax included a house, wharf and was a water lot. It must have been large enough to sell portions of it, as he sold a building lot for 1000 lbs. to Milcher Rhodes, a Sailmaker, in 1816, and another lot to Francis Muncey, a Halifax merchant, for 225 lbs. in 1817.

John applied for land grants in several parts of Nova Scotia (one grant, in 1810, was for land in either Halifax or Hants County and it was a joint petition with his brother-in-law, Matthew Walker. The petition states that the land was granted to both. Walker and his wife had 8 children at the time. He was granted 500 acres in Hants County. John Gosbee was also granted 300 acres. At that time, 1810, he had a wife and three children.) Another land grant petition, dated 1811, asked for land in the Country Harbour area. It stated that Gosbee had a wife and one child. The discrepancy in the number of children from the Hants County grant could mean several things: two of the children had died, two of them were "on their own" or it could just be an error in writing. A further petition in 1816 states "wife and 5 children".

The land that Gosbee (and others) asked for in Country Harbour had previously been granted. In 1815, they asked that the land be escheated [(Ref 003)] and regranted to them. The family did move to Country Harbour and lived there for a number of years before migrating to other places. Some of them moved to Guysborough, and the area where many of them lived is shown on old maps and noted on Census', as Gosbieville, Gosbee Settlement or Gosbee Section. A Laurilliard cousin, Charles, and his family also migrated to Country Harbour, and were living there as late as 1909.

John Gosbee married 1st) Hannah Allen on Sept. 27/1795, at the Methodist church, Halifax, by Rev. Black. They were married for fourteen years when Hannah died on Aug. 27/1809. [Ref 1.9] Three months after her death, John Gosbee married 2nd) Martha Greenwood on Nov. 26/1809, at St. Paul's Anglican Church, Halifax. The sons of the family became ship builders or carpenters, and in particular, Henry and Charles built and owned many ships.

Children:

1.91) James John Muncey Gosbee b: Nov. 14/1811 d: 1854
1.92) John Henry Gosbee b: Oct. 18/1812
1.93) William Francis Gosbee b: Sept. 20/1814
1.94) Charles Gosbee b: @ 1819
1.95) Henry Gosbee b: Sept. 12/1822
1.96) George Calbeck Gosbee b: June 4/1816 d: 1870
1.97) Joseph Francis Gosbee b: 1825 Country Hbr.
1.98) Matthew Gosbee b: @ 1827
1.99) Martha Jane Gosbee b: Dec. 7/1829

~~

1.91) James J. Gosbee married Agnes Osborne (b:1815), daughter of Robert and Agnes Osborne of Scotland, on October 8/1837, at Halifax by Rev. T. Taylor. [Ref 1.91] They lived in Guysborough, where James was a Ship Captain. In March, 1854 he left Halifax for the West Indies in the brig, ***Plover***, and was not heard from again. [Ref 1.91a] There are several recorded deeds and Release of Dower transactions involving Agnes, dated 1856. She migrated, with her children to the USA, where she was shown as a widow on the US 1870 Census for Boston/Ward Two. Agnes died on Apr. 28/1872 at Melrose, Mass., USA, of cancer.

Children:

1.911) Agnes Gosbee b: Sept. 28/1840
1.912) John Greenwood Gosbee b: Feb. 16/1842
1.913) James Osborne Gosbee b: Nov. 10/1843
1.914) Mary L. Gosbee b: @ 1847

1.915) James Albert Gosbee b: Dec./1851
1.916) Philip K. Gosbee b: Oct. 29/1853
1.917) Caroline M. Gosbee b: @ 1854

~

1.911) Agnes Gosbee married William J. Silver, a Sailmaker of Sackett Hbr., NY, (his 2nd marriage), in Boston in 1866.

1.912) John G. Gosbee migrated to San Jose, California. He married Annie Laurilliard, daughter of Albert and Annie (Osborne) Laurilliard. They had no children. Albert Laurilliard was a cousin who also migrated to San Jose, California. John G. Gosbee died on Mar. 16, 1888 at age 46 and is buried in Oak Hill Memorial Park in San Jose (Ref 1.912)

J.G. Gosbee
Died March 16, 1888
Aged 46 years & 1 month
A Native of Guysborough, Nova Scotia

1.913) James Osborne Gosbee – No further information, but probably died young, as another child born in 1851 was given the name James.

1.914) Mary L. Gosbee married George M. Tufts, son of Henry and Jane Tufts, on Nov. 30/1871 at Boston.

Children:

1.9141) Alice Mary Tufts b: Sept. 30/1872
Married Theodore H. Tufts, son of Theodore W. & Elizabeth (Cram) Tufts on Sept. 22, 1913 at Melrose, Mass.
1.9142) George Ernest Tufts b: Sept. 15/1874

Married Flora Gertrude Kennett on June 10/1903 at West Somerville, Mass.

1.9143) Lillian Maude Tufts b: 1879
Married Harry Butters Hurd at Chelsea, Mass., on Sept. 30/1908.

1.915) James A. Gosbee, ***and***

1.916) Philip Gosbee migrated to Astoria, Oregon. James was a Carpenter, Philip a Blacksmith. They relocated to Alaska in 1894, as stated on the 1900 US Census. They, along with a John Anderson became partners in gold ventures, and staked claims at Cahoon Creek, Alaska. Another man, Moreau Burnett, boarded with them. None of them were married.

I can find no further record of James A. Gosbee.

Philip Gosbee received a life sentence for murder in the first degree, and entered McNeil Island Penitentiary in Washington, on Feb. 1/1901. He gave himself up at Porcupine, Alaska.[Ref 1.915a] After fifteen years, he was parolled, on March 17/1916.

Philip married Anna A. (Laurilliard) Gosbee, widow of John G. Gosbee, (his sister-in-law), on Jan. 31/1917 at Seattle, Washington. He committed suicide on June 22/1922, at Tacoma, Washington. [Ref 1.915b]

1.917) Caroline M. Gosbee married J. Frederick Fraser, a Trunk Maker, who was also born in Nova Scotia. His parents were Roderick and Sarah A. Fraser. They were married on Nov. 30/1871, at Boston.

Children:

1.9171) Agnes Fraser b: Jan. 27/1873
1.9172) Howard Roderick Fraser b: Sept. 30/1875
1.9173) Roy Phillip Raeburn Fraser b: Jan. 29/1879

1.92) John H. Gosbee was a Ship Carpenter and became a Captain of vessels. He married Sarah Ann Street, daughter of Samuel Street, tailor, on May 15/1837, by Rev. Mr. Hamilton at the Brunswick Street Methodist Church. (Ref 1.92)

Children:

1.921) Martha Jane Gosbee	b: Feb. 24/1838
1.922) James Henry Gosbee	b: Oct./1839 Halifax
1.923) William John Gosbee	b: May 15/1840
1.924) Henry Manuel P. Gosbee	b: Dec. 7/1844 at Country Harbour
1.925) Nathaniel Gosbee	b: Dec. 26/1846 at Country Harbour d: Dec. 29/1849 bur. Hfx
1.926) Charles Greenwood Gosbee	b: March 14/1849 Hfx.
1.927) Samuel Smith Gosbee	b: @ 1856
1.928) Isaiah Washington Gosbee	b: July 15/1858
1.929) Harriet Jost Gosbee	b: Nov. 13/1860

~

1.921) Martha Gosbee married **1st)** Joseph McNeil, who was a Boot and Shoe Maker in Guysborough. On the 1871 Census, this family was shown with 7 **children:**

1.9211) Mary McNeil	b: 1859
1.9212) Harriet A. McNeil	b: 1860
1.9213) George McNeil	b: 1862
1.9214) Sarah McNeil	b: 1864
1.9215) John McNeil	b: 1866
1.9216) Margaret M. McNeil	b: 1868
1.9217) Charles McNeil	b: 1870

Joseph McNeil must have died soon after the 1871 Census. Martha married **2nd)** Lawrence Phelan/Phalen, farmer, of Riverside, on Aug. 6/1873. He was a son of John and Mary Phelan. Martha died between 1881 and 1891, as Lawrence is shown as a widower on the 1891 Census. The 1881 Census shows the McNeil children: George, Sarah, John, Margaret, and Charles with the surname Phalen.

Children:

1.9218) James Phalen b: 1875
1.9219) William Phalen b: June/1876 d: Nov.26/1951

1.9212) Harriet McNeil married Amos Ingersoll in Boston, on Jan. 31/1880. They had children Louisa A. Ingersoll and Frances H. Ingersoll (who married Holden A. Evans, a US Naval Officer). (Ref 1.9212)

1.9216) Margaret M. McNeil married **1st)** Thomas Addison, a Journalist, born in Aiken, South Carolina, on Dec. 23/1886 in Boston, Mass. They divorced, and she married **2nd)** Adelbert E. Hoyt of Chicago, a real estate broker, on June 10/1899 at Boston. They had two **children.** She became a Christian Scientist Practitioner at Brockton, Mass.

1.9217) Charles McNeil married Carrie Neary, daughter of John and Mary (Levinge) Neary, in Manhattan, New York, on Oct. 4/1894.

1.9219) William Phelan married Annie MacDonald, daughter of Alex. And Margaret (MacEachern) MacDonald of Antigonish County. They had **children:** Lawrence Alexander, Joseph W. A., James, Martha, Margaret Hilda, Charles Ira, John M.B., Thomas W., Mary Katherine.

~

1.922) James Henry Gosbee was a carpenter. He married **1st)** Mary Elizabeth Acker, on July 19/1866, at Guysborough. She was a daughter of John and Rachel Acker, of Guysborough. Mary Elizabeth died, aged 22, at Hartz Point, Shelburne County, on Apr. 19/1870. He married **2nd)** Charlotte Rollison at Shelburne in Jan./1870, daughter of George and Ann Rollison. Charlotte died, aged 24, on Dec. 23/1871. A 3 day old baby boy died on Dec. 20/1871. He married **3rd)** Delina Ross of

Shelburne on Jan. 14/1872. She was born on Cape Sable Island, to James and Elizabeth Ross. He married **4th)** Caroline Crouse, widow, in 1885. James Henry Gosbee died in December/1919, age 80.

Children:

1.9221) daughter b: Sept. 25/1867
Hartz Point, Shelburne County
1.9222) daughter b: March 24/1870
1.9223) son b: Dec. 20/1871
1.9224) Kinsman David Gosbee b: Aug. 19/1874 d: infant
1.9225) Kinsman Narraway Gosbee b: 1875
1.9226) Mary Ella Gosbee b: Mar. 24/1870
d: Feb. 18/1943
1.9227) Althea Blanche Gosbee b: July 20/1874
1.9228) Geneva Evelyn Gosbee b: 1878
1.9229) Melissa Palmer Gosbee b: 1881

On the 1901 Census, twin **granddaughters** Grace and Blanche, born 1899, lived with this family. They migrated to Lynn, Mass. and in 1920 Grace was a stenographer for an electric company, while Blanche was a stitcher in a shoe factory.

~

1.9225) Kinsman Narraway Gosbee was a carpenter. He married **1st)** Angelina McLeod at Shelburne, on Dec. 10/1898. She was aged 19, born at Sandy Point, a daughter of Arthur and Elora McLeod. The marriage was witnessed by Melissa C. Gosbee. Angie died on Feb. 4/1917, of T.B. at Shelburne. He married **2nd)** Arabella G. Wrent, a widow, aged 44, in 1914. She was a nurse. Her father was George Chapman, born Derbyshire, England. Kinsman died on Nov. 16/1958, age 88.

Children:

1.92251) Anzo May Gosbee b: @ 1899

Married Guerdon Foster Wesley, who was a 42 year old Shoemaker, and was a widower. She was 32. They married at Shelburne on Mar. 13/1931. (States her parents names as Kenneth Gosbee and Angeline MacLeod).

1.92252) Kinsman Gosbee b: @ 1902 d: of TB aged 15 years on Nov. 25, 1917, at Shelburne.

1.92253) Sherlock Holmes Gosbee b: @ 1904. He married Beatrice May Crowell on June 18/1926, at Shelburne. He was a carpenter. **Children:** Shirley, Burton, Danny, Sherlock Jr. (1940-2010)

Sherlock Holmes Gosbee, Jr.

1.92254) Robie Stanley Gosbee b: 1906
Married Gertrude Oikle of Shelburne, in 1932.

1.92255) Randolph Gosbee b: @ 1908
d: Dec. 5/1916, of T.B., at Shelburne.

1.92256) Hattie Glenora Gosbee b: ?
Married Harold C. Cunningham on Jan. 29/1926, at Shelburne. She signed the marriage certificate, "Miss Hattie Glenora Gosbey". They had a son, Harold Sherlock Cunningham, b: July 21/1929, d: Aug. 20/1996 at San Diego, USA.

1.9226) Mary Gosbee married John Seaboyer, a 60 year old widower, on Apr. 29/1908.

1.9227) Althea Blanche Gosbee married George R. Tupper on July 3/1901. He was a Telegraph Operator, a son of Capt. Oliver and Mary Tupper of Port Medway. They lived in Yarmouth, NS.

1.9228) Geneva Evelyn Gosbee married Worten Andrews Hathaway, son of Burnham A. & Mary (Thomas) Hathaway, of Machias, ME. They were married at Swampscott, Mass., on Aug. 25/1900. **Son:** Arthur Burnham Hathaway, b: Apr. 4/1903, Lynn, Mass.

1.9229) Melissa Palmer Gosbee married Paul Thibeau, on May 6/1901. He was a seaman, born Arichat, N.S. @ 1875, and resided in Boston, USA. His parents were Stephen & Sebine Thibeau. **Children:** Paul Bernard Thibeau, b: Oct. 28/1903,at Boston, and Mabel Thibeau, d: an infant on Nov. 7/1905.

~

1.923) William Gosbee married Elizabeth Ann Delaney, daughter of Patrick and Elizabeth (Dort) Delaney, of Sandy Cove (now Dort's Cove), on January 18/1867. She was born on Jan. 11/1845, and died on Oct. 14/1937.

Children:

1.9231) Martha Jane Gosbee	b: Mar. 10/1869	
1.9232) Sarah A. (Anna) Gosbee	b: 1872	
1.9233) Margaret I. Gosbee	b: Oct. 15/1871	
1.9234) William Joseph Gosbee	b: Dec. 2/1875	
1.9235) Mary E. Gosbee	b: May 15/1877	
1.9236) Alonzo James Gosbee	b: 1881	d: age 18
1.9237) John James Gosbee	b: Apr. 30/1882	
1.9238) Armenia Gosbee	b: Aug. 28/1884	
1.9239) George Gosbee	b: May 24/1887	
1.923 10) Alice Gosbee	b: July 28/1890	
1.923 11) Maggie A. Gosbee	b: Nov. 14/1897	

Annie (Delaney) Gosbee

Annie Delaney was a tall woman whose strength was legendary. It is said she could easily lift heavy, filled barrels onto a wagon by herself.

1.9231) Martha Gosbee married Waldo Howland. She died in Pawtucket, Rhode Island, on Aug. 4/1936.

Children:

1.92311) Bertha May Howland b: Aug. 20/1901
1.92312) Harry Allen Howland b: Feb. 25/1904

1.9232) Sarah Ann (Annie) Gosbee married William Byron Gould in 1892. He was a son of Israel and Ann (Goldsmith) Gould of Amherst, N.S. (Ref 1.9232)

Children:

1.92321) William Alden Gould b: August 12/1894
1.92322) Elizabeth S. Gould b: July 31/1896

1.9233) Margaret Gosbee married Henry McAuley, a widower with a daughter, Elizabeth McAuley. They had three more **children:**

1.92332) Queenie Mae McAuley – married Charles Hopkins.
1.92333) George McAuley
1.92334) James McAuley – married Lena Paupin.

1.9234) Joseph Gosbee married **1st**) Eliza Elmira (Rhynold) Cook, widow of Elias Cook, Roachvale, on September 20/1898. Her parents were James and Margaret (Hayden) Rhynold, of Little Dover.

R to L: Joseph Gosbee, son Les Gosbee, grandson Bill Gosbee holding his son Brian Gosbee.

Eliza had children from her previous marriage: Violetta, Harriet L. (Hattie, b: 1886), who married W. Wesley Sangster of New Harbour; Mabel Elizabeth (b: 1892), who married Thomas Jones of Roachvale; Ethel Victoria who married **1st**) John Shorten of Ogden, **2nd**) Thomas Marshall (b: Pictou, lived in Toronto) and Esther Jane (Essie), who married Stephen Kennedy.

Children of Joseph and Eliza:

1.92341) Martha Ann Gosbee b: @1899, who married 1st**)** Hugh Burns on Aug. 26/1919, at Guysborough. The marriage license states his employer "Dominion Police Force, Halifax", and his birthplace as Glasgow, Scotland. His father was a musician. She married **2nd**) James Parker, of the Musquodoboit area, and they operated The Parker House for many years. They had one **son**, William (Burns) Parker.

1.92342) Harry Garfield Gosbee b: Apr. 27/1903, who married Violetta May Sangster, daughter of Wesley and Hattie (Cook) Sangster of New Harbour, on Aug. 22/1932, at Trinity Church Manse, New Glasgow. At the time of their marriage, they were both living in the Barney's River area. They had a large family.

1.92343) Wilfred Laurier Gosbee lived at Cook's Cove. He had a long common-law relationship with Frances Peart. No children.

1.92344) Joseph Morton Gosbee who married **1st)** Margaret Laurella Hendsbee, daughter of Daniel and Mary (Grover) Hendsbee of Half Island Cove, on June 11/1928. She was age 17, he 21. She died, age 23, of pneumonia following an emergency appendectomy, in Antigonish, on May 30/1935. They had children. Joseph married **2nd)** Lillis Clattenburgh. They had children, including a daughter, Muriel Elmira Gosbee, born May 7/1945, who died aged 7 months on Dec. 26/1945.

1.92345) Agatha Hazel Gosbee b: 1914, d: 2003. She married **1st)** ___Attwood, **2nd)** Bruno Turcotte. She had children.

1.92346) Elizabeth Anna Gosbee b: @1894 At age 17, she married Frederick Edward Mitchell on July 18/1913, at Bible Hill. He was aged 22, born at Elmsdale, and worked as a Brakeman in Truro.

1.92347) Leslie Melrose Gosbee married Helen Bertha Purdy. They had children, including a daughter Joan Elizabeth Gosbee, born June 5/1937, died June 11/1937.

Joseph, Martha and Wilfred Gosbee

Agatha (Gosbee) Turcotte

Les and Helen Gosbee

Joe and Laurella (Hendsbee) Gosbee

Joseph and Eliza divorced,(Ref 1.9234). and he married **2nd)** Lexie Maria Worth, aged 22, on June 28/1927. She was from North Ogden, a daughter of Edward and Catherine (McCallum) Worth.

Children of Joseph and Lexie:

1.92348) William Edward Gosbee married Leah Hilchie (four children).

1.92349) George Ernest Gosbee died an infant.

1.9234 10) John James Gosbee married Amy Hendsbee (five children).

1.9234 11) Victor Allan Gosbee married Ruby Hilchie (five children).

1.9234 12) Bertha Christine Gosbee married Harry Silver (three children).

1.9234 13) Stella Odessa Gosbee married Gordon MacLeod and had children.

1.9234 14) Margaret Elizabeth Gosbee married Murray Zwicker. No children.

~

1.9235) Mary E. Gosbee married Ralph Waldo Harrington, son of Edward and Laura Harrington of Groton, Mass., on Mar. 25/1903. She died of Puerperal Septicaema on May 6/ 1905, at Groton.

~

1.9237) John Gosbee married (Elizabeth) Bessie Munroe on Feb. 26/1904. She was a daughter of Harriman and Margaret

Munroe of Cole Harbour. They lived in the Hazel Hill area, moving to New Waterford, where he became a coal miner. He died on March 30/1949. His death certificate gives a birth date of Apr. 25/1884. **Children:**

1.92371) Beatrice Annie Gosbee b: Apr. 29/1907, d: 1992. She married John P.T. Hall, migrated to Maine, then New Hampshire & is buried in Massachusetts.

1.92372) Alonzo James McAuley Gosbee b: 1910

1.92373) Hazel Gosbee b: ?

1.92374) Percy Gosbee, who married Ruby Burns and had children John Gosbee, and Percy Gosbee.

~

1.9238) Arminia Gosbee married George Peart. She died in 1914, age 31. They had one son, William (Billy) Peart, who married Marian Lucy "Edith" MacNeill of Cape Breton, and had children, including a son, Bill Peart, who died in 2011.

~

1.9239) George Gosbee married Sarah Blackburn at St. Ann's Church, Guysborough, on May 16/1907. He was 18, she was 17. Her parents were John and Catherine (McIsaac) Blackburn of Giant's Lake, although the marriage record states she was born at Lochaber, Antigonish County. He died at age 23 of "Inflammation of the brain", on Sept. 23/1911 at Tompkinville. They had a **child:**

1.92391) Annie Frances Gosbee b: Nov. 25/1908 (Ref1.92191)
She became a teacher. She married Daniel Michael McEachern in 1931 in Boston, Mass. He was born in Antigonish County. They had 10 children. (Ref1.92191a)

~

1.923 10) Alice Gosbee married **1st)** Walter C. McNutt, son of Charles and Julia McNutt of Truro, on Dec. 23/1909. He died in 1913, aged 22.

Child:

Dorothy Alice McNutt b. Oct. 25/1911 d. March 7/1912
buried Watson Cemetery, Truro.

Alice married **2nd)** John Long.

~~

1.924) Henry Manuel Gosbee was a carpenter/farmer. He married Margaret Roberts, daughter of John and Rebecca (Hattie) Roberts on January 25/1869. She was born on Aug. 3, 1843, and died on July 12/1932. Henry died on Aug. 9/1932.

Children:

1.9241) Henry James Gosbee b: Feb. /1875 d: Feb. 15/1926
1.9242) Sarah R. Gosbee b: @ 1879 No further info.

1.9241) Henry Gosbee was a carpenter. He married Lillian F. Lucas, daughter of Mary Lucas.

Children:

1.92411) Minnie Margaret Gosbee b: 1900
1.92412) Alexander Gosbee b: 1902
1.92413) Harry Francis Gosbee b: 1904
1.92414) Katherine Eva Gosbee b: 1908
1.92415) Evelyn Anastasia Gosbee b: 1909
1.92416) Arthur Gosbee b: 1910

1.92411) Minnie Margaret Gosby never married. She died in New Glasgow, on Dec. 11/1936.

1.92413) Harry Francis Gosbee married Winnifred Spanks, daughter of Alexander and Sarah (Munro) Spanks of Roachvale. They had a large family.

1.92414) Katherine Eva Gosbee (Katie), age 17, married James Anthony Kenny, a Steelworker, age 23, at New Glasgow. He was born at Country Harbour, a son of Robert H. and Olive (Walsh) Kenny. (Robert Kenny was born at Salmon River.) They were married on Nov. 13/1924.

~

1.926) Charles G. Gosbee married Amelia Cook, daughter of Francis and Ellen/Ella Cook, on Dec. 22/1873. He was a Mariner. This family migrated to USA @ 1890, and were living there in 1920, where Charles was an elevator operator in a Shoe Factory in Beverly, Mass. **Children:**

1.9261) Charles John Gosbee b: Nov. 23/1874
1.9262) Mary Ella Gosbee b: @ 1879
1.9263) Harriet L. Gosbee b: Nov. 13/1874
1.9264) Isaiah Gosbee b: Jan. 29/1883
1.9265) George Alfred Gosbee b: April 29/1885
1.9266) Levi James Gosbee b: July 12/1888 d: 1958

See notes at back regarding this family [GR 1.926)]

1.9261) Charles Gosbee married Eva May Nickerson on Aug. 24/1899. He was a seaman. She was born at New Harbour, a daughter of Levi and Lucy Nickerson. They migrated to Gloucester, Mass. And were living there at the time of the 1910 census, where he was a cook on a fishing vessel. By 1920, they lived in Lynn, Mass. Charles was a Stock Fitter in a shoe factory, as was his son James, while Eva kept a Lodging House. Daughter Ethel was a bookkeeper in a shoe factory. Son Robert was a Wireless operator on a steamship.

Children:

1.92611) James Leonard Gosbee b: Dec. 25/1899
1.92612) Ethel B. Gosbee b: @ 1902
1.92613) Robert Gosbee b: @ 1904
1.92614) Hattie Lillian Gosbee b: 1906 d: Oct./1906
1.92615) Stillborn son b: Apr. 11/1908

~

1.9262) Ella Gosbee married Joseph Robert Melanson, a Teamster, on Apr. 19/1902 at Gloucester. He was a son of Benjamin and Ellen (Thibodeau) Melanson.

Children:

1.92621) James A. Melanson b: 1904
1.92622) Herman Russell Melanson b: Nov. 3/1905
1.92623) Ralph W. Melanson b: 1910
1.92624) Melvin R. Melanson b: 1914
1.92625) Charles A. Melanson b: 1915
1.92626) Gilbert S. Melanson b: 1917
1.92627) Gladys A. Melanson b: 1918
1.92628) Margaret M. Melanson b: 1922

1.9263) Harriet L. Gosbee married 1st) Albert L. Allen, a fisherman who was born in Stonington, ME., USA., on Feb. 5/1908, at Gloucester, Mass. He was a son of Chase and Carrie (Clark) Allen. She was a widow by 1920.

Children:

1.92631) Albert L. Allen b: 1909
1.92632) Althea Allen b: 1911
1.92633) Charles Allen b: 1912
1.92634) Cora Allen b: 1913
1.92635) Laurena Allen b: 1915

Harriet married 2nd) Percy C. Smith. They lived in Beverly, Mass.

1.9264) Isaiah Gosbee never married. He was a cook aboard fishing schooners. At the time of the 1911 census, he was age 65, living with his brother Henry in the Shelburne area. The family consisted of Henry's twin granddaughters, Grace and Blanche, and a Zwicker family, who were listed as boarders.

1.9265) G. Alfred Gosbee was a Printer/Typesetter. He married Velma Gross, daughter of John and Mary (Alliston) Gross of Yarmouth, NS, on Feb. 4/1912.

Children:

1.92651) Daughter b: May 17/1915
1.92652) Phyllis M. b: Dec. 19/1927

1.9266) Levi (Lee) Gosbee migrated to the Beverly, Mass., USA area. He married Pearl A Stone (who had a son Allen W.)

Child:

1.92661) Merrill Lee Gosbee b: Nov. 28/1920
d: June 23/1988

~

1.927) Samuel Gosbee married Rebecca Elizabeth Roberts, daughter of John and Rebecca (Hattie) Roberts of Guysborough, on Aug. 20/1888. She was a sister to Margaret Roberts, who married Samuel's brother, Henry. She died on March 16/1941.

Children:

1.9271) Hugh Aupolis Gosbee b: May 31/1892
1.9272) Gordon Alexander Gosbee b: Jan. 18/1894
d: Feb. 5/1955
1.9273) Murray Garfield Gosbee b: Oct. 16/1895
1.9274) Hilda Hattie Rebecca Gosbee b: Jan. 29/1898
1.9275) Alonzo Edward Tupper Gosbee b: June 6/1901

1.9271) Hugh Gosbee emigrated to the USA and became a naturalized citizen in 1923.

1.9273) Murray Garfield Gosbee married Mary Elizabeth Peart and had children.

1.9274) Hilda Hattie Rebecca Gosbee married Ira Washington Andrews, son of John and Harriet (Gosbee) Andrews on Jan 5/1932, and had children.

~

1.928) Isaiah Gosbee was a cook aboard ships, and was a crew member on the *Esperanto* when she became the first winner of the International Fishing Vessel Championship, on November 1/1920 .[Ref 1.924]

~

1.929) Harriet Jost Gosbee married John William Andrews on Dec. 10/1878. He was a carpenter and farmer, son of David and Jane Andrews, and a descendant of Isaac Andrews, one of the Hallowell Grant Settlers. **Children:**

1.9291) Sarah Anne Andrews	b: 1880
1.9292) George Andrews	b: 1881
1.9293) Samuel David Andrews	b: 1882
1.9294) Martha Jane Andrews	b: 1884
1.9295) Ada Andrews	b: 1887
1.9296) Guy Andrews	b: 1890
1.9297) Elizabeth M. Andrews	b: 1893
1.9298) Ira Washington Andrews	b: 1895
1.9299) Margaret Andrews	b: 1897
1.929 10) Delbert Andrews	b: 1900
1.929 11) Amelia Andrews	b: 1902
1.929 12) John Henry Andrews	b: 1905

1.9291) Sarah A. Andrews married Edward James Alexander Hull, carpenter, son of John and Margaret Hull of New Harbour. They were married on Oct. 2/1899.

1.9293) Samuel David Andrews never married. He died at age 56.

1.9294) Martha Jane Andrews married Edward Lucas, son of Lawrence and Anastatia (Farrell) Lucas of Guysborough.

1.9298) Ira Washington Andrews was a farmer. He married Hilda Hattie Rebecca Gosbee (1.9274), daughter of Samuel and Elizabeth (Roberts) Gosbee.

1.9299) Margaret Andrews married Charles Stanley Cresine in 1919. He was the son of James and Jennie Cresine of Havendale.

1.929 11) Amelia Andrews married Charles Lucas, son of Lawrence and Anastatia Lucas, and a brother to her sister

Martha's husband, Edward Lucas. He was 34, she was 16, at the time of their marriage.

1.93) William Gosbee married Mary MacPherson. They lived at Cape Canso.

Children:

1.931) William Frederick Gosbee	b: Jan. 1/1851
1.932) John Joshua Gosbee	b: Sept./1853
1.933) Joseph Edmund Gosbee	b: July 29/1856
1.934) Lewis/Louis Alonzo Gosbee	b: July 31/1861

1.933) Joseph E. Gosbee married Margaret E. Grady, daughter of William and Mary (Chisholm) Grady . She was b: July 4/1865 at St. Francis Harbour, NS. (Ref 1.933). Joseph was an Oil Clothes Maker, and lived in the Canso area. Joseph and Margaret adopted a son: Nathaniel, born Jan. 29/1895. Nathaniel Gosbee married Jean Horne, daughter of William and Amelia (David) Horne, in 1918. (She was a widow, aged 18). Nathaniel died prior to 1925, when Jean Gosbee, widow, married Norman Haskell Levy on Dec. 11/1925, in Halifax. Joseph E. Gosbee died on Jan. 10/1919, and his widow, Margaret, married Thomas Hearn in 1922, at Star of the Sea Church, Canso.

~

1.934) Lewis Gosbee never married. He was a fisherman out of Gloucester, Mass. at the time of the 1900 census, which was taken on June 9th of that year. From a list of Nova Scotia fishermen lost at sea whose names appear on a memorial in Gloucester, Mass. - ***Lewis Gosbee, 37, single, Canso. Sigfrid at Sable Island, October 12, 1900.***

1.94) Charles Gosbee had a livery stable in Guysborough, as well as being an Expressman, as listed on the A.F. Church map Subscribers Directory. His home, and also the home of his son, Charles, are shown on the map, at the far northern end of Church Street, in the area of Guysborough that was sometimes called Gosbieville or Gosbee Settlement. He married Louisa Cook, daughter of John and Mary (Cameron) Cook, on Jan. 28/1845.

Children:

1.941) Charles Archibald Gosbee	b: 1849	d:1903
1.942) Marshall Gosbee	b: June 4/1851	
1.943) Alma Louisa Gosbee	b: March 25/ 1853	
1.944) Caroline Ada Gosbee	b: Jan. 8/1857	
1.945) John C. Gosbee	b: @ 1860	
1.946) Maria (or Eliza M.) Gosbee	b: April 1/1863	
1.947) Mary Elizabeth Gosbee	b: Feb. 22/1846	

GUYSBOROUGH
BUSINESS DIRECTORY.

Hon. Stewart Campbell. Judge of County Court
E. I. Cunningham, J.P. Custos and Postmaster
James A. Tory, J.P...... Collector of Customs
James E. Hart............ C.C.C. and Registrar of Probate
H. R. Cunningham & Son, Dry Goods, Groceries, &c.
Rufus A. Tremain ... Barrister-at-Law; Lloyd's Agent; Receiver of Wrecks
J. W. C. Grant .... Hotel Keeper
Charles Gosbie............ Livery Stable and Expressman

A.F. Church Map, circa. 1873:

Charles Gosbie.......

Livery Stable and Expressman

1.941) Charles Archibald Gosbee was a ship builder. He married 1st) Charity Esther Carr on Dec. 16/1873, at Ragged Head. He married 2nd) Martha <u>Letitia</u> Scott in 1884. She was born on Dec. 4/1865, a daughter of William G. and Martha Scott. She died at North River, NS, at the Colchester County

Home, aged 69, on Aug. 30/1934.

Children:

1.9411) Harold Storey Gosbee	b: Jan. 17/1886	
1.9412) Gertrude L. Gosbee	b: Aug. 6/1888	
1.9413) Katherine Louise Gosbee	b: May 23/1891	
1.9414) Wilbur Scott Gosbee	b: Apr. 19/1892	
1.9415) Clarissa Gosbee	b: Oct. 20/1895	
1.9416) John W. Gosbee	b: May 15/1899	d: 1980
1.9417) Frank Mitchell Gosbee	b: Feb. 12/1902	

1.9411) Harold Gosbee was living in Amesbury, Mass. In 1910, where he was a metal worker in an auto body manufacturing plant. He boarded with the family of John J. and Agnes Scott.

1.9412) Gertrude L. Gosbee married Harold A. Biddle of Glens Falls, NY, USA, son of Joseph R. and Alta B. (Clark) Biddle, on July 17/1907, at Greenfield, Mass.

1.9413) Katie Gosbee married Sherman G. Conary, son of Edmin F. and Grace L. (Palmer) Conary of Blue Hill, ME., on June 23/1911, at Chelsea, Mass.

1.9414) Wilbur Scott Gosbee was an electrician. He enlisted in the Canadian Army in WW I at North Vancouver, N.C. His mother was living in Chelsea, Mass. at the time. He married Edith Violet Fox on July 12/1921. She was born in Scotland, a daughter of George and Christina Fox. Wilbur died on Mar. 2/1977.

1.9415) Clarissa Gosbee married Roy M. Graves, son of Julius and Ada E. (Spaulding) Graves, on July 5/1913, at Springfield, Mass.

1.9416) John W. Gosbee migrated to USA and lived in the Chelsea, Mass. area in 1918. He was a member of the

Masonic Lodge of Hampden. He married Ann Steiner. They had a son, John W. Gosbee, who married and had six children, including a son, (Dr.) John W. Gosbee.

1.9417) Frank Mitchell Gosbee married Ruth ____.

~

1.942) Marshall Gosbee married Sarah J. Kennison, daughter of James and Sarah A. (Welch) Kennison of Prince Edward Island. They lived in Gloucester, Mass. He was lost from the ***Mystic*** off Louisbourg on April 19/1892. She remarried in 1893, to Benjamin Nelson, a Swedish fisherman.

Children:

1.9421) Edward M. Gosbee (Gosby) b: 1876
1.9422) Annie L. Gosbee b: Jan. 23/1882
d: age 3, tubecular meningitis
1.9423) Ella M. Gosbee b: 1880
1.9424) Charles Gosbee (Gosbey) b: 1875 d: 9 mos.
1.9425) Mary E. Gosbee (Gosbey) b: Feb. 24/1878

1.9421) Edward M. Gosbee (Gosby) married Mary E. Hodgdon, daughter of John C. and Sarah D. (Saunders) Hodgdon of Gloucester, on Jan. 26/1903. He died in 1922. (Ref1.9421)

Child:

1.94211) Edward Marshall Gosbee b: June 29/1903

1.9423) Ella M. Gosbee married Fay L. Hazard, a Motorman, son of Royal E. and Nellie L. (Bowen) Hazard, of Sheldon, VT. They were married in 1907 in Boston.

~

1.943) Alma L. Gosbee married Frank Burton Muncey, merchant, of Gloucester, Mass. On Aug. 24/1876. She died on July 9/1881, at Gloucester, age 26.

Child:

1.9431) Willie F. Muncey b: 1878 d: Mar. 26/1881

~

1.944) Caroline Gosbee married Miles Jorden. He was a blacksmith, who was born at Sherbrooke, N.S. This family lived various places throughout Guysborough County.

Child:

1.9441) Frank Muncey B. Jorden b: @ 1879

~

1.945) John Gosbee - From a list of Nova Scotia fishermen lost at sea whose names appear on a memorial in Gloucester, Mass. - ***John Gosbee, 44, single, Guysborough, washed overboard W.H. Moody at Georges Bank, Jan. 25, 1905.***

~

1.946) Maria Gosbee married Frederick Lewis, son of Willard and Belinda Lewis of Booth Bay, Maine, on Jan. 13/1882, at Salem, Mass.

~

1.947) Mary Elizabeth Gosbee married William H. Leet, a blacksmith, son of Andrew and Margaret (Bass) Leet of Guysborough, on Mar. 14/1869 at Gloucester. She died on Dec. 19/1913, at Providence, R. I. At the time of the US 1900 census, she was living alone with a grandchild, Ethel Chambers, age 5. It was stated that she was the mother of 4 children, only 1 still living at that time. **Children:**

1.9471) Anna M. Leet b: 1870
1.9472) Willie V. Leet b: 1872 d: 1908
1.9473) Hattie W. Leet b: 1876 Married J. R. Chambers

1.95) Henry Gosbee married **1st)** Ann Rebecca Toby, daughter of Joseph and Ann (Murphy) Toby, on Jan. 11/1848. He married **2nd)** Eveline Wheaton of Guysborough on Sept.

6/1864. She was born in the U.S.A.

Children: *The first 5 were by mother Ann Rebecca. Some of the children of this family spelled the surname GOSBEY, others, GOSBEE. On the A.F. Church Map for Mulgrave area – Subscribers Directory – Henry GOSBIE is listed as Ship Carpenter and Mail Contractor, circa 1873. (See Ref 1.95 for more details).*

1.951) Elizabeth Anne Gosbee	b: 1850
1.952) Elisha Henry Gosbee	b: Aug. 7/1851
1.953) Joseph Levi Gosbee	b: 1854 Carpenter
1.954) Emma Maria Gosbee	b:1857 Dressmaker
1.955) Arthur S. Gosbee	b: 1860
1.956) Edward James Gosbee	b: 1866 Carpenter
1.957) George Gosbee	b: 1867 Farmer
1.958) Harriet L. Gosbee	b: 1868
1.959) John Francis (Frank)Gosbee	b: 1871 Carpenter
1.95 10) Lucretia Christina Gosbee	b: Dec. 25/1872
1.95 11) David Murray Gosbee	b: Jan. 11/1876
1.95 12) Perley Gosbee	b: 1878
1.95 13) Clara Estella Gosbee	b: Nov./1881

1.951) Elizabeth Anne Gosbee lived with her mother's family at Cook's Cove (Tobys) at the time of the 1871 Census. She married Godfrey Wheaton.

Children:

1.9511) Effie Lorenda Wheaton	b. Oct. 23/1879
1.9512) Emma May Wheaton	b. Oct. 11/1881
1.9513) Charles Henry Wheaton	b. Aug. 2/1886
1.9514) Guy Wheaton	b. 1889

1.9512) Emma May Wheaton married Stanley Morton Horton on June 21/1905.

1.9513) Charles Henry Wheaton married Marie Elizabeth Fitting. He died in Vancouver, B.C., on Aug. 2/1886.

~

1.952) Elisha Henry Gosbee was a mariner. He married Emma Cole, daughter of John N. and Sarah Ann (Ford) Cole, of Liverpool, NS., at Gloucester, Mass., on July 29/1879.

Children:

1.9521) Joseph Levi Gosbee b: @ 1880
1.9522) Elizabeth Octavia Gosbee b: @ 1884
1.9523) Ella M. Gosbee b: May 28/1885
1.9524) Willis A. Gosbee b: 1891 d: Aug.10/1892
1.9525) Carlos Cole Gosbee b: Aug. 30/1896 d: 1970
1.9526) Henry B. Gosbee b: Sept. 7/1881 d: 1916
1.9527) Annie E. Gosbee b: June 30/1883
1.9528) George Bryant Gosbee b: Aug. 14/1889
d: Jan. 20/1950
1.9529) Ida L. Gosbee b: 1887
1.952 10) Ernest Osier Gosbee b: July 19/1901

1.9521) Joseph Levi Gosbee (age 31) married Ethel Evangeline Bishop (age 19), daughter of Freeman and Louise (White) Bishop of Kentville, NS. They were married at Gloucester, Mass., on May 14/1911. They later moved to Maine. **Children:**

1.95211) Audrey Louise Gosbee b: 1911
Attended Waltham Training School for Nurses in 1930.
1.95212) Raymond Gosbee b: Dec. 22/1913
1.95213) Phyllis Gosbee b: 1916

1.9522) Elizabeth Octavia Gosbee married Edward Burton Giles, son of Smiley and Agnes (Wood) Giles, on July 1/1913, at Cambridge, Mass.

1.9525) Carlos Cole Gosbee married Sarah Ethel Rath, daughter of James and Catherine (McMunn) Rath (b: 1897, d:

1933). They are buried at Fort Pierce, Florida.

1.9528) George B. Gosbee married Isabelle Winona McArthur, daughter of Isaac W. and Darenda J. (Graham) McArthur, on Apr. 8/1908, at Worcester, Mass. **Child:**
1.95281) Roland Elwyn Gosbee b: Oct. 31/1908

~

1.954) Emma Maria Gosbee married Horatio N. Irving, Ship Joiner, who was born at Port Mulgrave, NS, son of William and Jane (Scott) Irving. They were married in Gloucester, on June 29/1892.

~

1.955) Arthur S. Gosbee was a Ship Carpenter. He married C. Annie B. McInnes, daughter of Donald and Almira McInnes, on June 27/1883, at Peabody, Mass. They had no children.

~

1.956) Edward James Gosbee died Oct. 1/1941, in the Pictou/New Glasgow area. Never married.

~

1.958) Harriet L. Gosbee married Hubert Moors, who was born in Newfoundland, son of Richard and Elizabeth (Parsons) Moors, on Oct. 8/1908, at Gloucester, Mass.

~

1.95 10) Lucretia Christina Gosbee married John Allen MacDonald on Sept. 7/1899, at Mulgrave. They were both 26 years old at the time of their marriage. He was born at Mira, Cape Breton, and was working as the Canadian Express Manager at Mulgrave (Railroad). Later years, they lived in Stellarton.

~

1.95 11) David Murray Gosbee never married. He died Nov. 12/1952 in Sydney, NS. He had been a Marine Fireman for the NS Government. His nephew was Hubert MacDonald, Sydney.

~

1.95 12) Perley Gosbey married **1st**) Agnes Mabel Urquhart, on June 8/1904, at Stellarton. He was a Brakeman. He migrated to Vancouver, B.C. Where he married **2nd**) Jennie May Lewis, daughter of Theodore Harding and Mary Elizabeth (Hatt) Lewis. He died on Jan. 12/1952. **Child:**

1.95 12 1) Lloyd Otis Gosbey b: July 25/1919

Married Roberta Morrison. He died on Jan. 10/1986 at Vancouver, BC.

1.96) George C. Gosbee was a Shipwright. He married Eliza W. Scott on March 15/1845. She was a daughter of John and Maria Scott, of Guysborough, NS. They migrated to Essex, Mass. She died of heart disease at age 47, on Oct. 6/1865 at Essex. He died in 1870, age 58.

Children:

1.961) Mary C. Gosbee b: @ 1846
1.962) John Scott Gosbee b: March 20/1848
1.963) Sarah Eliza Gosbee b: June 1/1851
1.964) Gorham Marchant Gosbee b: May 31/1854

1.961) Mary C. Gosbee married George W. Knowland, son of George and Sarah L. Knowland, on June 30/1869, at Essex, Mass.

~

1.962) John S. Gosbee married Hannah E. Blake, daughter of Hubbard and Mary E. Blake of Rockingham, New Hampshire, on March 9/1871.

~

1.963) Sarah Eliza Gosbee (Sadie) married Fernando Albert Gove, son of Abdon and Eliza W. Gove in 1871 at Gloucester, Mass.

Children:

1.9631) Gertrude W. Gove b: 1874
1.9632) Ernest P. Gove b: May/1875
1.9633) Grace G. Gove b: Sept. 10/1887

~

1.964) Gorham Marchant Gosbee migrated to Minnesota and was working on a farm in the Acoma area @ 1880.

1.97) Joseph Gosbee married **1st)** Maria McKeough, daughter of John and Ruth McKeough. They emigrated to Essex, Mass, where he was a shoemaker. She died at age 28, three days after giving birth to stillborn twin girls on April 14/1852. He migrated to California, settling in Pacific Grove, Santa Clara County where he was the first shoemaker. (Ref 1.97) He married **2nd)** Sarah Frances Smith, daughter of Ansyl Smith, on July 3/1856. (Ref 1.97a) Joseph died in 1915, age 84, at the home of his son Perley, in San Jose. (Ref 1.97b)

Children:

1.971) Carrie Luella Gosbey b: Aug. 15/1857
1.972) Perley Francis Gosbey b: May 15/1859
1.973) Hattie Verna Gosbey b: Sept. 1/1865
d: Jan. 14/1867
1.974) Herbert Austin Gosbey b: May 10/1868
d: June 19/1868
1.975) Stella May Gosbey b: Apr. 24/1869
1.976) Joseph Stanley Gosbey b: Mar. 16/1874

1.971) Carrie Luella Gosbey married Rev. John Jeffrey Martin on June 12/1884. They lived in Auburn, California.

~

1.972) Perley Gosbey was elected a Judge of the Superior Court of Santa Clara County, California. He married Susan Rucker, daughter of Joseph E. and Susan (Brown) Rucker, on October 28/1891. (Ref 1.972)

Perley F. Gosbey

~

1.975) Stella M. Gosbey was a teacher. She married Baron D. Merchant on April 24/1889. They lived in Oakland, California. No children.

~

1.976) Stanley Gosbee married and had a son Homer S. Gosbey. They lived in San Francisco. Stanley was listed as a widower on the 1910 Census. Homer was age 11.

1.98) Matthew Gosbee was born in Country Harbour. He married Hannah Glen from Guysborough Intervale on Nov. 14/1849. (Ref1.98) This family moved to the Canso area and then later to Murray Harbour, Prince Edward Island. Matthew died in May/1882. Hannah died in Essex, Mass. In 1891. All the children were born in Nova Scotia.

Children:

1.981) Albert Whidden Gosbee	b: Sept./1850	
1.982) Thomas O. Gosbee	b: Oct. 20/1852	
1.983) John M. Gosbee	b: 1856	d: Mar. 18/1913
1.984) Joseph Dimock Gosbee	b: 1856	
1.985) Matthew E. Gosbee	b: 1858	

1.986) Georgina Gosbee b: 1861
1.987) Mary E. Gosbee b: 1863
1.988) David Henry Gosbee b: Dec. 24/1865
1.989) Barbara Maria Gosbee b: Aug. 25/1867
d: Feb. 11/1868, typhoid fever

1.981) Albert W. Gosbee was a Ship Carpenter. He married **1st)** Rebecca Rude (b:June 15/1849, daughter of Alex and Hannah (Marine) Rude), on Dec. 8/1874. They migrated to the Gloucester area, where they had one **child**:
1.9811) Frederick A. Gosbee b: June/1881

Albert married **2nd)** Mary (Elliott) King, widow, on Oct. 6/1917, at New Glasgow. She was born at Lyons Brook on Mar. 28/1864, and died on May 3/1939. The marriage certificate gives his residence as Gloucester, Mass., and his occupation as Sea Captain. The marriage was witnessed by Pearl and Mrs. Pearl Gosbee. Her parents were Thomas E. and Elizabeth (McKenzie) Elliott. (She had children prior to her marriage to Albert W. Gosbee, including son Milton V. King.) Albert died in Aberdeen Hospital, New Glasgow, on Dec. 20/1926. His death record gives his birthdate as Feb./1849, in PEI.

1.9811) Frederick A. Gosbee married Maude E. Noble, daughter of William B. and Letitia F. (Gould) Noble, on Jan. 22/1903. They lived in Gloucester, Mass. **Children:**
1.98111) Evelyn Maud Gosbee b: July 20/1903
1.98112) Frederick Glenn Gosbee b: Jan. 6/1906
1.98113) Richard Otis Gosbee b: Apr. 19/1908
1.98114) Robert Gould Gosbee b: Jan. 22/1915

1.98112) Frederick Glenn Gosbee was a Private in the US Army, inducted from Mass., and was a Private in the Medical Dept. He was lost at sea on May 10/1944.

His name is among those on the
Tablets of The Missing at Honolulu Memorial.

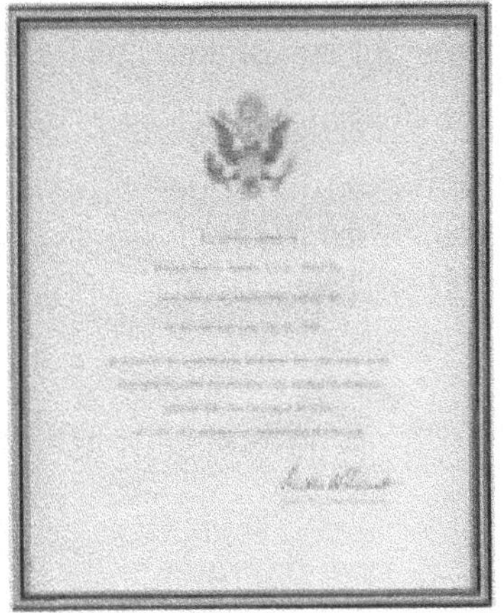

The Certificate reads:

IN GRATEFUL MEMORY OF
Private Fred G. Gosbee,
A.S. No. 31231230,
WHO DIED IN THE SERVICE
OF HIS COUNTRY
in the American Area, May 10, 1944

HE STANDS IN THE UNBROKEN LINE
OF PATRIOTS WHO HAVE
DARED TO DIE THAT FREEDOM
MIGHT LIVE AND GROW, AND
INCREASE ITS BLESSINGS.

FREEDOM LIVES, AND THROUGH IT,
HE LIVES – IN A WAY THAT HUMBLES
THE UNDERTAKINGS OF MOST MEN.

Signed: Franklin D. Roosevelt
President of the United States of America

~

1.982) Thomas Gosbee was a seaman and became a sea captain. He married 1st) Sarah Ann Wheaton on Nov. 19/1877. She was a daughter of Edward Cornwallis & Janet Wheaton of Guysborough, NS. He married 2nd) Annie C. Jewers, of Beaver Harbour. Thomas died on July 6/1935.

Children:

1.9821) Laura Gosbee b: 1879
1.9822) Hannah R. Gosbee b: 1880 d: 1956
1.9823) Thomas Osborne Gosbee b: 1888
1.9824) Caleb Grafton Gosbee b: Dec. 12/1894 d: Jan. 20/1974
1.9825) Sarah E. Gosbee b: 1883 d: May 17/1886

1.9821) Laura Gosbee married George Jordan, widower, age 45, who was a "Railroad man". He was born at Guysborough, son of Andrew and Ann. She was 29, daughter of Thomas and Sarah, and born at Murray Harbour, PEI.

1.9822) Hannah Gosbee married Benjamin Jenkins of Peters Road, PEI.

Children:

1.98221) Grafton Lovell Jenkins b: Apr./1902
1.98222) Raymond Thomas Jenkins b: Apr./1903
1.98223) Foster Wheaton Jenkins b: Dec./1908 d: 1957

1.9823) Thomas O. Gosbee married Harriet Caroline (Hattie) Penny of Cape Bear, PEI.

Children:

1.98231) Florence Harriet Gosbee b: Oct. 23/1923
(married Kimball Frederick LeLacheur on Nov. 1/1945)
1.98232) Louis James Gosbee b: Sept. 6/1914 d: 2010
1.98233) Charles Grafton Gosbee b: 1920 d: Feb. 6/2008
1.98234) Lovell Thomas Gosbee b: 1922 d: Aug. 29/2010
1.98235) Elmer Cecil Gosbee (married Vaughn Moore)
1.98236) Dorothy Gosbee (married Clifford Jackson)
1.98237) Ruth Gosbee (married Lloyd Waldo Hawkins)
1.98238) William W. Gosbee b: May 3/1910 d: 1972
(married Jean B. MacLeod)
1.98239) Murray Clair Gosbee b: Nov. 29/1927
d: Apr. 16/1987
1.9523 10) Sadie Gosbee (married Ray M. Bell)

1.9824) Grafton Gosbee enlisted in WWI, in the NS Regiment, returning from overseas on May 16/1919, aboard the ***Olympic.*** He married Annie Isabelle Robertson (1898-1999).

Children:

1.98241) Reuben Gosbee b: 1920 d: Sept. 28/1944
Private, Cape Breton Highlanders, KIA, WWII
Buried in Cesena War Cemetery, Italy
1.98242) Jimmie Gosbee b: June/1930 d: Nov./1930
1.98243) Clara Mae Gosbee b: 1937 d: 2004
Married Ernest Larry Brown and lived in Cornwall, Ont.

~

1.983) John Gosbee was a seaman. He married Dorcas Letitia Grant (b: 1859, d: Feb. 13/1923), daughter of Abijah and Dorcas (Bears) Grant, and a sister to Catherine Ann Grant, who married his brother Dimock. This family lived at Gladstone, P.E.I. **Children:**

1.9831) David Henry Gosbee b: 1884 d: 1946
1.9832) Mabel Gosbee b: March/1881
1.9833) Annie Gosbee b: @ 1883
1.9834) Alexander Matthew Gosbee b: Mar. 28/1885 d: May 3/1959
1.9835) Clara E. Gosbee b: Nov. 13/1886
1.9836) Mercy Gosbee b: @ 1889
1.9837) Mary L. Gosbee b: 1891
1.9838) John Alonzo Gosbee b: Apr. 29/1897
1.9839) Catharine A. Gosbee b: @ 1880

1.9831) David H. Gosbee married Sarah Nettie Moore (1886-1970). **Son:**
1.9831) William N. Gosbee.

1.9834) Alexander M. Gosbee married Catherine M. MacLean (b: Apr. 25/1882, d: Nov. 4, 1968). **Children:**

1.98341) Annie Catherine Gosbee b: Feb. 27/1911 d: Feb. 6/1974
1.98342) John Alonzo Gosbee b: August 19/1915 d: May 28/1991
1.98343) Lenora May Gosbee b: Dec. 10/1909

1.98344) Helen Letitia Gosbee b: Sept. 7/1912
1.98345) Francis Russel Gosbee b: June 15/1917
1.98346) Lloyd George Gosbee b: Feb. 13/1919

1.98342) John Alonzo Gosbee was a Signalman in The Royal Canadian Corps of Signals, World War 2. He married Sybil Dorothy Herring, the daughter of James F. and Mary Jane (Gordon) Herring, on March 1/1941. *Their grandson, George F. J. Gosbee, was one of Canada's Top 40 Under 40 in The Globe and Mail's Report on Business. He is the founder of Tristone Capital Inc.* (Ref 1.98342)

1.98346) L. George Gosbee married Helen Vuozzo.

1.9835) Clara Gosbee married William Buell on Nov. 20/1901. She died July 22/1944.

1.9838) John Alonzo Gosbee enlisted in the Canadian Army in WWI, in 1915, at Charlottetown, P.E.I. He married Anna (Annie) Lowe at Halifax, on Sept. 4/1918. They had a son Michael Francis who died at Halifax in 1923, age 2.

1.9839) Catharine A. Gosbee married Edward J. Elliott, a Teamster, who was born at Pictou, NS, son of George and Isabell (Johnson) Elliott. They were married on July 18/1900, at Boston.

~

1.984) Joseph Dimock Gosbee was a seaman in his early years, beoming a Bridge Builder later on. He married **1st**) Catherine Ann Grant, daughter of Abijah and Dorcas (Bears) Grant (Ref1.984a)of P.E.I. This family migrated to USA, but Catherine left and returned for a time to P.E.I., taking the children with her. Joseph D. hired Pinkerton's Detective

Agency to kidnap his son, Matthew, and he was taken back to his father in Massachusetts. (Ref 1.984)

Joseph D. married **2nd**) Margaret McDonald, daughter of Alexander and Ann McDonald of Pictou, NS, on July 11/1890 in Portland, Maine. She died age 52 on Oct. 24/1906, and it was she who raised Matthew.

Joseph D. married **3rd**) Mary J. Pratt (Shearer), who was born in England, a daughter of William and Christina (Russell) Shearer. They were married on Nov. 7/1910 at Everett, Mass. He died at Everett, on June 6/1916.

Children:

1.9841) Georgina Gosbee b: Feb. 17/1879
1.9842) Dorcas Letitia Gosbee b: Dec. 6/1880
1.9843) Matthew Gosbee b: 1889

* A *William* Gosbee was born July 22, baptised on Oct. 20/1899 to this family. Was this another of Matthew's names?

1.9841) Georgina Gosbee married **1st**) Richard William Silliphant, son of Richard and Flora (McKinnon) Silliphant of Prince Edward Island. She married **2nd**) Albert Lorne Ross, a moulder, born in P.E.I., son of Daniel F. and Priscilla J. (Glenn) Ross, on Aug. 18/1902, at Cambridge, Mass.

1.9842) At age 11, Letitia Gosbee lived at the home of John W. and Mercy Horton, whose home was next door to her mother and sister, who were living with Abijah and Dorcas Grant, her grandparents. Lettie married Herbert Snell, son of Herbert M. and Maria (Bonney) Snell, on Nov. 19/1902, at Somerville, Mass. **Children:**

1.98421) Herbert Nathan Snell b: Aug. 22/1903
1.98422) George Albert Snell b: Feb. 14/1905 d: 1910
1.98423) Irving G. Snell b: 1908
1.98424) Edith C. Snell b: Sept. 9/1909

1.9843) Matthew Gosbee was brought up in the USA. He became a minister. He married Ella Mae Lane and had four

sons:

1.98431)	Wilber Clyde Gosbee	b: 1925	d: 2009
1.98432)	David Gosbee	b: 1929	d: 2004
1.98433)	Paul Gosbee	b: 1930	
1.98434)	Kenneth Irving Gosbee	b: Aug. 4/1932	d: 2010

~

1.985) Matthew Gosbee was a carpenter. He married Julia Worth (1862-1943), on May 24/1882, at Boston. She was born in Nova Scotia, the daughter of William and Mary Worth, who migrated from Cape Breton to Pugwash, NS. Matthew and Julia's children were born in USA, but they returned to Prince Edward Island in 1890. (Ref 1.985) Matthew was struck and killed by a train in Oakland, California in 1909. By 1911, Julia was living at Pictou Island with widowed daughter Mabel and grandson Roland A. MacPherson (b: PEI). Julia was working as a cook in a factory.

Children:

1.9851) Perley William Gosbee b: Jan 27/1883
d: Apr. 21/1942

1.9852) Mabel Lillian Gosbee b: Aug. 28/1884

1.9851) Perley William Gosbee married Jessie Mae Court (b: Aug. 31/1892, d: May 6/1942).

Children:

1.98511) Ethel Mae Gosbee b: 1922 d: 2007
(married John Sidney Moore July 18/1945)

1.98512) Robert Gosbee b: July 20/1918
d: May 18/1977

1.98513) Mildred J. Gosbee b: ? d: Mar. 11/1975
(married Elmer Glover)

1.9852) Mabel Gosbee married ____ MacPherson.

Child:

1.98521) Roland A. MacPherson b: Feb. 10/1910
d: Oct. 3/1983

(Married Laura Mae Roberts)

~

1.986) Georgina Gosbee married Murdock MacPherson, who was born in Scotland, the son of Peter and Ann (Beaton) MacPherson of Glasgow. [Ref 1.986] They lived in Manhattan, New York, USA, and at the time of the 1920 census, nephew Matthew Gosbee lived with Georgina, who was a widow. She later married Abraham Hankin. Murdock MacPherson was a painter and paper hanger, as well as a "street preacher". There were a number of marriages between members of the Gosbee family with MacPhersons, including Georgina's brother, David, who married Murdock's sister, Flora.

Children:

1.9861) Albert MacPherson b: Aug./1884
1.9862) Murdock MacPherson b: Feb./1886
1.9863) Frank MacPherson b: Feb./1888
1.9864) Stella MacPherson b: Jan./1889
1.9865) Glenn MacPherson b: July/1890
1.9866) Donald MacPherson b: Oct./1892
1.9867) George MacPherson b: Mar./1894
1.9868) Margaret MacPherson b: Feb./1896
1.9869) Walter MacPherson b: Nov./1899
1.986 10) Georgina MacPherson b: 1903

Georgina and son Walter MacPherson

Georgina and Abraham Hankin

~

1.987) Mary E. Gosbee married Joseph Hemmeon Myers, son of Isaac and Catherine Maria (Hadley) Myers of Guysborough, at Gloucester, on April 30/1887. They had no children. He died on March 25/1903. She worked as a tailoress, as shown on the US 1910 census, and was listed as a Practical Nurse on the 1920 census, at Essex.

~

1.988) David H. Gosbee was a carpenter. He migrated to Essex, Mass. in 1882. He married Flora McPherson, who was born in Scotland.

Children:

1.9881) Florence Gosbee		b: Dec. 18/1888	
1.9882) Annie May Gosbee		b: @ 1889	
1.9883) Hannah Glenn Gosbee		b: 1890	d: 5 mos.
1.9884) Joseph H. Myers Gosbee		b: Jan. 21/1892	
1.9885) Albert Roy Gosbee	***TWIN***	b: Mar. 22/1894	

1.9886) Ralph Owen Gosbee ***TWIN*** b: Mar. 22/1894
1.9887) David Earl Gosbee b: Oct. 7/1898

1.9882) Annie May Gosbee married Theodore R. Grimsley, a Machinist from Charlotte, NC., USA., on Apr. 24/1909, at Everett, Mass. He was a son of Patrick and Picket (Kendall) Grimsley.

1.99) Martha Jane Gosbee – No further information

REFERENCES

Most vital statistics and census records are available online through various websites. I used Ancestry.com, Nova Scotia Historical Vital Statistics, FamilySearch.org, AmericanAncestors.org (through NEGS), FindAGrave.com, and various other regional online sources.

(Ref 001) Online Source - http://www.surnamedb.com/surname.aspx?name=Gosby

(Ref 002) Early Journalism in Nova Scotia - Advertising Columns of the Gazette of 1772 - Page 111: Collections of the Nova Scotia Historical Society, Vol. 4-6.

(Ref 002a) St. Paul's Anglican Church Records, Halifax. Burial of John Gosbee, April 16/1777. Burial of Mrs. Elizabeth Gosbee (widow) age 67 years, on Dec. 3/1799.

(Ref 003) Escheat - When property and/or an estate is transferred to the government because a person has died without a will or an heir to his or her estate. Original granted lands were often abandoned, thus available to be re-granted to another person.

(Ref 004) The Foreign Protestants and the Settlement of N.S. - Winthrop Bell.

(Ref. 005) ~ A mantua is a woman's long cloak.
~ Bacchus was the god of wine and revelry, son of Jupiter and Semele.

(Ref. 1.4) Seth and Sarah Webb lived in the Dutch Village area of Halifax, where they farmed, and later moved to Hants County. Seth was buried on Apr. 23/1793, age 43.

Some of their children were: Joseph Webb (b: 1774); Mary Webb (b: 1777), Jane Webb (b: 1780); Lydia Webb (b: 1783); Seth Webb (b: 1785); William Webb (b: 1787). Their son, Seth, married twice: 1st to Margaret Clark and 2nd to Frances Amelia Chandley on Jan. 4/1838 at St. Paul's Church, Rawdon. They lived in Windsor.

They had many children, including: John **Gosby** Webb (b: 1822); John A. Webb (who was a Sail Maker); Sarah Webb (who married Joseph A. Kilcup); Mary Elizabeth Webb; Susan Webb (who married Harris M. Caldwell).

John Gosby Webb and William Webb were druggists at Windsor. There are many discrepancies in some of the branches of this family. The above names and dates were found in various transcribed church records. Many more details and other family members are available for further research.

(Ref 1.9) Nova Scotia Royal Gazette: Tuesday, 29 Aug./1809

(Ref. 1.9a) John was a Captain of vessels as well as a Shipwright. There are records of Captain John Gosbee of the schooner Jane & Martha, from 1812-15, from Halifax to P.E.I & Magdalen Islands. (Ex: Weekly Recorder 19 Sept., 1812: arrived Schooner Martha, Captain Gosbee, from Halifax, passenger Lieut. Alex Mcdonald of H.M. Canadian Regt. of Glengary Sharp Shooters on recruiting service.)

(Ref 1.91) Acadian Recorder: Saturday, 14 Oct./1837

(Ref 1.91a) Harriet Cunningham Hart – *History of the County of Guysborough*: Page 94. Page 92 also mentions another mishap where James Gosbee was the captain: The first Guysboro and Halifax packet to make regular trips was the schooner *Sylph,* in 1847, owned by E.I. Cunningham. In 1848, when, near the entrance to Halifax Harbor, she was cast ashore on Devil's Island and became a total wreck. All on board were saved.

Steve Wright of Guysborough wrote a song about Captain James Gosbee, titled ***Skipper Jim:***

Born in Shiretown Guysborough Nova Scotia,
Grew up on decks of schooners all around the bay
Skipping rocks and skipping school, some said he was bound to be a fool
But he knew in his heart what he'd become someday
And he heard all the Captain's stories of the lands far beyond the sea
He dreamed of the day he'd have a schooner of his own
And all the town folk then would call him ***Captain James Gosbee***
At twenty one he married, a new wife and his son

At twenty four they had three more oh they were so in love
He worked for merchant seamen catching fish off Newfoundland
He could stoe a hold like no man and number one deck hand
He worked hard saved his money; Bought a house with a harbour view
And every time he'd go away he'd take her in his arms and say
Listen to this song I sing, don't be sad and I love you
(CHORUS)
He sang blow ye winds high ho
A roving I will go
Across those stormy seas
But my love soon I'll be
In your arms again
I'm your Skipper Jim
After years of climbing that ratline of success
As Captain of the packet Sylph, his will be put to test
Lying hard for Halifax in the gale of '48'
They smashed upon Devil's Isle, but all the crew were saved
Mary said, "Jim I need you here, please think of our children too"
Oh Mary dear I live this dream and I know it's hell on you
But separate a man from dream
He'll end up on Dog Lane too
Well twenty years of sailing Skipper Jim always came home
He built a brig the ***Plover*** and he traded fish for rum
He sold that little house and planned a mansion on the hill
He said "I'll have it built while I'm at sea on my last trip I'll sail"
I've waited for this for years she said, "A life with you my man."
And standing on the timbers of the dreams that they had laid
She listened to him singing
As he sailed out the bay
(CHORUS)
Well the sea's a cruel harsh master, there is no guarantee
A life time of hopes and dreams can end in tragedy
She was seen upon the widow's walk looking out for miles around
But the papers read left widow, and six children in the town
But Mary stayed up there watching;
Wind swept tears streaked across her face
You promised us we'd have a life together at the end
She gripped the rail and cried out,
"Damn you Skipper Jim"
Well the packet brought a letter dated March of '54
She opened it and read it as she'd done oft times before
We're loaded up in Halifax and we're West Indies Bound
I'll see you in a month or two if everything goes well....
She broke down by her window; It had been a year and she still grieved

The P.S said I miss you and I'll be with you soon
Don't forget about the song I sing,
Don't be sad and I love you
..and she could hear him singing...
(CHORUS)
Then she sang:
Blow the winds high ho
A roving I will go
Across those stormy seas
But my love soon I'll be
In your arms again
You're my Skipper Jim

To hear a clip of this song: **http://www.eswright.com/music-28.html**

(Ref 1.912) Online: http://www.findagrave.com # 55126535

(Ref 1.915a) ***Victoria Daily Colonist***, Tuesday, Jan. 15/1901:
The trial of Phil Gosbee for murder is going on at Juneau. Gosbee was indicted for killing old man Campbell at Porcupine last July. Gosbee admitted the killing when he surrendered himself to the officers of the law, but will defend himself at the bar of justice on grounds that have not yet been disclosed.

The Washington Post, Jan. 29/1907:
An application was made to the President yesterday for the pardon of Capt. Phil Gosby, who is serving a life sentence at McNeil's Island, Wash., for the murder of a man named Campbell, at Porcupine, Alaska, six years ago. The application was presented by Gov. Hoggatt of Alaska, and Jack Dalton, the famous "musher" and winter traveler of the early Klondike days.

Fairbanks Daily Times (Fairbanks, Alaska) Aug. 10/1916:
Washington, D.C., Aug. 9 --- President Wilson today amended the civil service rules so as to permit paroled prisoners in the federal penitentiaries to fill civil service positions. The order was the result of an effort on the part of the department of justice officals to provide work for Phillip Gosbee, a prisoner at McNeil Island. Gosbee was convicted of murder as the result of a dispute of an Alaskan mining claim and was sentenced to life imprisonment.

The Washington Post, Aug. 10/1916:
Wilson Issues an Order Amending the Civil Service Regulations. ....The order was the direct result of an effort on the part of Dept. of Justice officials to help Philip Gosbee, a 63 year old prisoner in the McNeill Island Penitentiary, Washington, who was convicted of murder in a dispute over an Alaskan mining claim in February, 1901, and sentenced to life. Gosbee had filled a position in the mechanical dept. of the prison many years without pay, and it was decided to give it to him after his parole, but the civil service rules had to be amended.

McNeil Island Penitentiary Records give the following details: Born Guysborough, Nova Scotia. Vertical Scar over left eye. On right fore-arm tattoo of "*Young America*", on left fore-arm "*Independence*". Reads, Writes, age 48, 5 feet, 9 ½ inches, weight 128, brown hair, fair complexion, blue eyes, occupation Blacksmith.

(Ref 1915b) His Parole was "Terminated by Reason of Suicide" June 22/1922. Washington Death Certificate: Film # 1992969 Digital GC# 4221438, Image #704 Vol/Page CN566. Phillip Gosbee, died June 22/1922, Tacoma, Pierce, Washington. Age at death 69 years, 7 months, 24 days. Parents: James Gosbee, Agnes Osborne. Spouse: Anna A. Gosbee.

(Ref 1.92) Acadian Recorder – Saturday 27 May/1837

(Ref 1.9212) Holden Evans, born in 1871, and Academy graduate, determined early to become a Naval Constructor rather than stay in the line. He admitted that the career change "would give me some independence, one in which I can make my living in civil life." Sent to Glasgow, he studied under Archibald Barr, who would later become involved in the development of rangefinders for big guns. He represented the new group of engineers who were trying to achieve recognition in the navy after 1890. *Holden A. Evans, One Man's Fight for a Better Navy (New York: Dodd, Mead, 1940)*

*I*n the decade before World War I, two American naval officers tried to reform naval manufacturing with the help of Frederick W. Taylor, the foremost management consultant of his time. They failed. Admiral Caspar F. Goodrich was forced to retire in 1909, and

Commander Holden A. Evans resigned in 1911 after his career was ruined for trying to change a Navy organizational policy by implementing Taylor's management ideas. Yet, the lengthy deliberations about how to manage helped the Navy find its own "best way" prior to World War I.

Holden A. Evans became the president and general manager of the Baltimore Dry Docks & Shipbuilding Company, Baltimore, where a ship bearing his name was christened by his daughter, Miss Iris Evans: *Marine Review: Volume 46 1916.*

(Ref 1.92191) Birth Registration N.S. : Registration Year: **1908** - Page: **58000085** - Number: **58000087**
At the time of her birth, the family was living in the Hardwood Hill area of Sydney, NS, where George worked as a teamster.

(Ref 1.92191a) Information received from Anne Blanchard (Grandaughter of George and Sarah).

(Ref 1.9232) William and Sarah migrated to the United States and settled in Massachusetts, first in Southboro, where they had a son named William Alden Gould, born August 12/1894. They then moved to Cambridge, Massachusetts. There they had a daughter named Elizabeth S. Gould on July 31/1896. Eventually they moved to Leominster, Massachusetts. William was a yard overseer in salvage recycling (according to a census record) and Sarah was a seamstress.

Sarah Ann Gosbee Gould committed suicide in the attic of her home on February 16/1916. She is buried in Evergreen Cemetery in Leominster, Massachusetts.

William Byron Gould is buried in a pauper's grave in St. Leo's Cemetery in Leominster.

Their son, William Alden Gould married Ora Virginia Morse (born June 6/1896 in Fitchburg, Mass, to William Henry Morse and Celina Mary Obie). William and Ora had two children, twins named Doris Mae and David Alden. The twins were born on November 7/ 1922. They were born and raised in Leominster, and graduated from St. Bernard's High School in Fitchburg, class of 1940. William Alden Gould died June 18/1974 in Leominster in a hospital. David married and had children. Their middle child was a girl, Janet Gould, and she was born on September 2/1955. She died September 17/2000 of breast cancer. David died on April 13/1993: *Information from Christine Lewin - daughter of Janet Gould.*

Ref 1.9234) Joseph and Lexie's marriage record, at New Glasgow states he is a Bachelor, age 49, but Eliza's death certificate shows Widow crossed out and Divorced written over it in black marker. (Court for Divorce and Matrimonial Causes, 1759-1960: RG39d, C408, Gosbee vs Gosbee, 1924) Eliza moved in with her son, Wilfred, and died at age 90 years, 2 months, on August 7/1958.

*Thanks to Gerald Gosbee for the photo of Joseph, son, grandson and great-grandson.

(Ref 1.924) International Fishing Vessel Championship, 1920: Under command of Captain M. Welch, *Esperanto* became the first winner of the International Fishing Vessel Championship on November 1/1920 when she beat the Canadian fishing schooner Delawana under command of Capt. T. Himmelman. Her crew included:

Isaiah Gosbee
Middle Left
Marked with X

Capt. Martin L. Welch, R. Russell Smith, **Isaiah Gosbee**, George E. Roberts, Harry P. Christianson, George Young, Benjamin W. Stanley, Roy P. Patten, Raymond McKenzie, James McDonald, Wallace Bruce, John Batt, John F. Barrett, Thomas Smith, Michael J. Hall, Stephen F. Whitney, Hugh Young, Benjamin H. Colby, James B. Connolly, John J. Matheson, Thomas S. Benham, Leon G. Murray, Lawrence F. Percival, Ernest Hendrie, Robert W. Sawtell, Morril Wiggins.

On May 30/1921, just months after winning the International Fisherman's Schooner Race in Halifax, Esperanto struck the submerged wreck of the "S. S. State of Virginia" off Sable Island, and sank. The crew manned Esperanto's dories and rowed away, and were eventually rescued. The skipper on that trip was Capt. Tom Benham. **Isaiah Gosbee**, the cook from the 1920 races, was among those aboard Esperanto that day.Attempts were made to salvage Esperanto, and she was actually raised by pontoons several times, but each time she slipped beneath the waves again. After a month of attempts, the efforts to raise her had caused such damage that the salvage operation was reluctantly halted.

(Ref 1.926) There are discrepancies in the names and birthdates of some of the children:

- Son John was born Nov. 23/1874 as per his birth record.
- Son Charles John who married Eva Nickerson in 1899 at age 22 makes his birthdate 1875 (as does one census record)
- Son John who married Mary Rose in 1905 was born in 1883. In looking at the other Johns with Charles as fathers, Charles who married Letitia Scott did so only in 1884, and Charles who married Louisa Cook did so in 1845. Unless the records give the mother's name in error, I cannot figure out which Charles is the correct one, but Charles and Amelia probably didn't have two sons named John. There is also a record of a unnamed son born to Charles and Ann (Cook) Gosbee on Dec. 21/1874.
- The US <u>1910 Census</u> for Gloucester lists JOHN, AMELIA, George, Levi, and ELLA as Mother in law, who was the mother of two children, both living. Also, Lillian Carver, niece, age 15, lived with this family.
- <u>List of Protestants in Isle Madame, January 1852</u>:

Cook	Francis	Fisherman	32
"	Ellen Luce		30
"	John		10
"	Amelia		8
"	Elisha		1

There are discrepancies in the ages on the List of Protestants which was supposedly written in 1852, and other Vital records.

(Ref 1.933) Information received from Terri Forbrigger.

(Ref 1.9421) July 11/1922 - Gloucester Daily Times: Edward M Gosbee, a Spanish-American War Veteran and a member of William McKinley Camp, United Spanish War Veterans, of this city , passed away early this morning at the Essex County Sanitarium, Middleton, where he was located for about three weeks receiving treatment after a lingering illness. He was 45 years 11 months 8 days of age. During the Spanish-American War he was an ambulance driver. He was employed for some time at the Grocery of Moses Babson and the Dolliver grocery on Main street and also at the bottling works of George A. Davis. He leaves beside his wife Mary E. (Hodgdon) Gosbee, one son Marshall Gosbee and his mother Mrs. Sarah Nelson , two sisters Mrs. Georgie E. Parsons and Mrs. Ella Hazard both of Boston.

(Ref 1.95) In 1879, James Carey and his wife Mary charged Henry Gosbee of Port Mulgrave with assault. They won the case; Henry went to jail, and his real estate and other items were sold at Public Auction to discharge the debt. His residence consisted of 1/6 an acre. Also sold were *1 red horse, 2 yearling heifer calves, 10 sheep, one old riding waggon, one old sleigh, 1 harness, 2 tons of hay*, etc.

(Ref 1.97) From ***Pacific Grove***, by Kent Seavey: He owned the Pioneer Boot and Shoe Store on Lighthouse Road. His home was across Lighthouse Road from the new Methodist-Episcopal church and assembly hall. A gregarious and outgoing sort from Nova Scotia, Gosbey rented rooms to visiting clergymen. Now known as the Gosby House Inn, the building has been in continuous use as a hostelry for over 100 years. Gosbey was a strong supporter of the church and a civic leader, serving on the board of trustees from 1892 to 1896.

(Ref 1.97a) From ***A Genealogical History of the Descendants of the Rev. Nehemiah Smith of New London County, Conn:*** by Henry Allen Smith

(Ref 1.97b) HISTORY OF SANTA CLARA COUNTY
Transcribed by Marie Clayton, from Eugene T. Sawyers' History of Santa Clara County,California, published by Historic Record Co. , 1922, page 529:

California owes much, as one of the most attractive corners of the world in which to live, thrive and be happy, to its distinguished members of the Bench and Bar, and prominent among whom may well be mentioned the Hon. Perley Francis Gosbey, Judge of the Superior Court of Santa Clara County, where he has made Department Two widely known for the high standards set in handling probate matters and the dispensation of justice.

He was born on May 15, 1859, at Santa Clara, the son of Joseph F. and Sarah (Smith) Gosbey who were married in 1856 . Mr. Gosbey, Senior, was born in Nova Scotia in 1825, came to California via Panama in 1853 and setttled in Santa Clara. He ran a hotel, called the Morgan House, in San Jose for a number of years, giving this up to engage in the shoe business, which he conducted for fifty years. He died in 1915 having ranched almost ninety years of age.

Mrs. Gosbey was born in Ohio in 1838, came to this state with her father, Ansyl Smith, crossing the Isthmus in 1852, and settled in Santa Clara; Mrs. Gosbey died in 1903. The later years of their lives Mr. and Mrs. Gosbey lived in Pacific Grove. There were two sons and two daughters in the Gosbey family, three of whom are still living.

Early view of Gosbey Boarding House before round turret tower was added to front. Colonial-style (eagle finial) streetlight reads: "1888 Gosbey House" on glass panes. c1890

Later view of Gosbey Boarding House at Lighthouse and 18th Street. Round turret tower added to front . c1899

In 1888, J.F. Gosbey, owner of Pacific Grove's first shoe store, opened his home to summer boarders, those visiting the old Methodist retreat. To house more guests, he added to the Queen Anne building several times, resulting in the inn's irregular plan.

Operating today as Gosby House Bed & Breakfast Inn, it has achieved National Historic Landmark status.

Perley F. Gosbey pursued the elementary courses and was graduated from the Santa Clara high school in 1875. He then went to the University of the Pacific, and there in 1880 he was given his Bachelor of Arts degree. In 1881 he began teaching school and for four years was a teacher in the San Jose high school. Thur far he had laid the foundation for future attainment; but how well in this preparatory work he had builded can can be seen in the success he has attained as a professional man.

Having decided upon the law as his future field, Mr. Gosbey went East to the University of Michigan and there matriculated in the Law Department; in 1888 he received his parchment and the degree of Bachelor of Laws. In June of that year he was admitted to the Bar at Ann Arbor, Mich.; and having returned to his native State, Mr. Gosbey was admitted, in the following Septemeber, to practice at the California Bar. In November, 1908, after years of private practice in which he had proven himself exceptionally qualified for work on the Bench, Mr. Gosbey was elected Judge of the Superior Court of Santa Clara County, and he has continued to hold that high office ever since.

On October 28, 1891, Mr. Gosbey was united in marriage with Miss Susan Rucker, the ceremony taking place at San Jose. Mrs. Gosbey is a daughter of Joseph E. and Susan (Brown) Rucker, born in Santa Clara County and a gifted and attractive lady who has more and more shared in the Judge's increasing popularity.

A preominent man in fraternal circles, Judge Gosbey is a Sottish Rite and Knights Templar Mason and a Shriner. He is a Past Grand Master of the Odd Fellows and Past exalted Ruler of the Elks and belongs to Observatory Parlor No. 177, Native sons of the Golden West and is a member of the California Pioneers of Santa Clara County. A native son, not merely in name but in the intensity of his patriotic spirit, Judge Gosbey has always been conspicuous for his public-spiritedness. For four years he was a member of the Board of Education of San Jose, acting as its president.

(Ref 1.97b) An Old Grove Pioneer Gone: Gosbey, Hon. J.F. - Monterey American, Feb. 23, 1915: Hon. J.F. Gosbey, formerly a resident of Pacific Grove, but for some years a resident of San Jose, has passed away at the home of his son, Judge Perley F. Gosbey, at the age of ninety-four years.

(Ref 1.972) Petition for Consideration of a Historical Property contract (California Mills Act) between the City of San Jose' and the owners of the Arguello-Gosbee House, City Landmark File No. HL06-

156, located at 456 North Third Street on a 0.2 acre site. ....Nestled among other single family homes, the Arguello Gosbey House, built for Camilla and Luis L. Arguello in 1890, is a notable structure in the locally and nationally recognized Hensley Historic District....This two and a half story residence is an exceptionally well preserved example of Queen Anne architecture........Luis L. Arguello was a prominent local real estate broker and native to the Santa Clara Valley. He was also the grandson of Luis Antonio Arguello, the first governor of Alta California after its independence from Mexico. Joseph Rucker, the following owner of the house, was the partner of Luis L. Arguello in the successful real estate firm Rucker & Co. ....Judge Perley F. Gosbey was a prominent local educator and jurist. He was the president of the San Jose Board of Education for the early part of the twentieth century and was elected Judge of the Superior court in 1908, a position he held until his death in 1937. (*Note - Perley F. Gosbey married a daughter of Joseph Rucker.*

(Ref 1.98) Hannah (Glenn) Gosbee was a daughter of Thomas and Mary (McKenzie) Glenn. Thomas Glenn was born in Ireland. Mary McKenzie was a daughter of James and Hannah (**Larabee***) McKenzie, who were both part of the group of people who arrived in Guysborough (then called Chedabucto or Manchester) in June, 1784, belonging to "The Associated Departments of the Army and Navy" at the end of the U.S. Revolutionary War.

**Hannah's parents were Isaiah and Barbara Larribee, who were Quakers. She and her brothers and sisters were part of the group of new settlers, although the other Larribees moved on to other places – John and Susan migrated to Mabou, Cape Breton.*

This group of settlers had previously landed at Port Mouton (near Liverpool, Queens County) in 1783, where they named their settlement Guysborough. The area was rocky and barren, and they barely survived the winter. Women and children were forced to stay inside tents and huts. In the spring, a fire destroyed all their homes and they escaped with only the clothes they were wearing. No written records survived. The decision to leave Port Mouton was made quickly and fishing vessels from Liverpool were hired to take the first contingent eastward to Chedabucto Bay. Some settled permanently (as did our ancestor, James) and the name was changed to Guysborough.

Two years' provisions were given to each person or family, which included food: flour, beef and/or pork, etc., building supplies, tools, farm implements, grain and seeds, tents, small boats, clothing and blankets.

James McKenzie was given a grant of land in Guysborough Intervale, near what is now Roman Valley, part of a huge section of land granted to the Associated Departments of the Army and Navy. A great-great-grandson, also James MacKenzie, lived on the original homestead lot, the fifth generation to do so (James to Asa to Donald to William to James, until his death a few years ago). There are records of twelve children born to James and Hannah McKenzie.

James McKenzie died before November/1835, when his estate was legally settled. The land had been divided into 9 shares of eighteen and one-half acres each, between his widow and 8 surviving adult children: Asa McKenzie, Annabella Nickerson, Bethany McCallum, John James McKenzie, Susan Davidson, Elizabeth Tory, Donald McKenzie and Hannah Lucas. Donald McKenzie and Hannah Lucas sold their shares of the estate to their brother, Asa, the previous year. (Their sister, Mary Glen, died in 1829.) The remaining six siblings also sold their shares to their brother Asa in 1835, for a total price of 50 pounds 10 shillings.

(Ref 1.98342) Biographical Notes, Department of Finance Canada - George F.J. Gosbee, Chairman, President and CEO, Tristone Capital:

George F.J. Gosbee founded Tristone Capital Inc. in September 2000. Prior to Tristone, Mr. Gosbee was a Managing Director at Newcrest Capital Inc., a Canadian national investment firm. Mr. Gosbee joined Newcrest after five years with the energy investment firm of Peters & Co. Limited, where he was a Managing Director and served on the Executive Committee.

Mr. Gosbee holds a Bachelor of Commerce degree from the University of Calgary. In 2004, Mr. Gosbee was named by The Globe and Mail's Report on Business as one of Canada's Top 40 Under 40. As well, for the past three years Alberta Venture Magazine has chosen him as one of Alberta's 50 Most Influential People. In 2005 Ernst & Young named him the Prairie Region Entrepreneur of the Year.

Mr. Gosbee is Vice Chairman of the Alberta Investment

Management Corporation, the $70-billion Government of Alberta fund. Mr. Gosbee is also Chairman of the Board for the Alberta College of Art and Design, and a board member of the Alberta Economic Development Authority, Edge School and the Libin Cardiovascular Institute of Alberta. He is a past board member of the Banff National Mountain Centre, the Sandy Cross Conservation Foundation and the Art Gallery of Calgary.

(Ref 1.984) Recollections of Ella Gosbee, received via Fred Gosbee of Maine, grandson of Matthew:

Catherine took the three children and left for PEI when Matthew was an infant. When Dimock returned he didn't know where they had gone and hired Pinkertons to find them and get Matthew, which they did. He was raised by Margaret in the Boston area. After Matthew died, my parents took Ella, my grandmother, to stay for awhile with relatives in New York state. On their return trip they stopped and visited Leticia, who was living at the time in Brookline, MA. That is where my mother heard the story of the Pinkerton kidnapping.

Lettie also said that in the latter years of her life Catherine frequently lamented about how they had stolen her baby. Lettie would have been about 10 years old in 1890, when the kidnapping took place, and would have, of course, heard the story from her mother.

(Ref 1.984a) July 30 1887 - Saint John Globe: On 17th inst., one of the most remarkable gatherings occurred at the home of Henry A. BEARS, Murray River, P.E.I. The mother,Mrs. Dorcas BEARS, the eldest d/o late Abraham WHITMAN of Canso, N.S., now aged 87 1/2 years, still enjoying all her faculties, was favored with the gathering of all her family of 13 children, who met for the first time to greet her as an unbroken family, except the father, who died some 14 years ago, aged 77 years. On Monday morn. an artist was secured and a picture of the family group was taken. The names and ages of the family are as follows: The mother, Dorcas BEARS, aged 87 years 6 mos.; James W. BEARS, 67 years 8 mos.; Sarah A. COOK, 66 years 3 mos.; Dorcas L. GRANT, 61 years 9 mos.; Abraham W. BEARS, 63 years; Mercy C. HORTON, 61 years 8 mos.; Isaac A. BEARS, 59 years 9mos.; David A. BEARS, 57 years 3 mos.; Rebecca E. COOK, 55 years 6mos.; Hannah E. CUDDY, 54 years; John F. BEARS,

51years 8 mos.; Henrietta J. BREHANT, 48 years 10 mos.; Henry A. BEARS, 45 years 6mos.; George W. BEARS, 43 years 6 mos. Making a total of 826 years,10 mos. The grandchildren are now 65 living and 28 dead; the great grandchildren are 73 living and 4 dead. There was present at the gathering a brother and sister of the father.

(Ref 1.985) ***Springfield Republican***, Feb. 2/1909:
While trying to dodge a train at Oakland, Cal. Yesterday, Mathew E. Gosbee of Boston was struck by an engine coming from the opposite direction and suffered injuries from which he died in a short time. ***Courtesy of Marjorie Osterhout.***

(Ref 1.986) Research on this family was done by Marjorie Osterhout.

The Laurilliard Family

The matriarch of the Gosbee family was Elizabeth Laurilliard. The name is found spelled various ways – Lorillard, etc. A brief and very incomplete sketch of the Laurilliard family follows:

LAURILLARD: *This name came from the Berenese Jura to Montbéliard in the 16th century. The first Loreillard (Lorillard or Laurillard) who appeared was Vernier Lorillard who became a citizen of Montbéliard in 1592. The family was there from at least 1586 when the father, Pierre, was already upon arrival "citizen of Porrentruy". At that time, the document tells us, he was "old, unable to travel or manage his affairs as in the past, and had seven children still alive". Vernier, one of the eldest, seens to have been the most attentive to the father. All the Laurillards were artisans or merchants: bakers, a butcher, a hotel keeper, a goldsmith and a tinsmith can be counted. In the 18th century, Charles-Jerémie Laurillard, stockingmaker, had issue including Charles Léopold, called Charles, born in 1783, who collaborated with the great Cuvier. All the numerous Laurillard family descended from Pierre Loreillard of Porrentruy. While the name has been widespread, its main location remained the Town of Montbéliard.* [LRef001]

Jean Christophe Laurilliard married **Anne Clement** on Sept. 8 or 9, 1734, in London, England. There are records of marriages - at Fleet Prison on Sept. 8, and at Westminster on Sept. 9. [LRef100] Daughter **Elizabeth** was born on April 30/1736, and baptised at Saint Anne's Church in Soho, Westminster, on May 2.

The Laurilliard family arrived in Halifax in 1749, via the ship ***BEAUFORT***. Jean Christophe Laurilliard (also referred to as John Christopher or Jonathan Christopher) born @ 1704 was listed as a husbandman, married with 2 boys and one girl at the time of his arrival.

The Last Will and Testament of John Christopher Laurilliard of Newport, Hants Co., mentioned his "Beloved daughter", **Elizabeth Gosbie**", as well as his "Beloved Son", **John Henry Laurilliard** and his "Beloved Son", **George Laurilliard**. John Christopher Laurilliard has a tombstone at St. Paul's Cemetery in Halifax. He was buried on Aug. 16/1786.

Elizabeth Laurilliard married John Gosbee, as his second wife.

John Henry Laurilliard married Sarah Lake. They had no children.

George Laurilliard was born @1749. He became a Ship Carpenter. There are records of several marriages - to Mary Fitzmorris in 1777, and to Mary Ford in 1788. There may be more. He died August 6/1815 , aged 66. He left a widow and 13 children. I can find record of eleven of them. In 1810, he and his older sons petitioned for land in Hants County. George Laurilliard's petition stated he "was born in England and came to Halifax with his parents as a child". Thomas Laurilliard was born in Halifax and is married, as is William, while Christopher is a single man. The first (George) has a wife and 8 children. (His sons who were also applying for grants would not be included in this number of children.) 1200 acres were subsequently granted, divided among them.

Descendants of George Laurilliard

L1) Thomas Hardwell Laurilliard b: @1776 d: Nov. 9/1830
L 2) Sarah Laurilliard b: @1785
L3) Henry Laurilliard b: @1790 d: 1899
L4) William Laurilliard b: @1790
L5) Edward Laurilliard b: @1792 d: 1793
L6) George E. Laurilliard b: @1799
L7) James Laurilliard b: ? d: 1801 Smallpox
L8) David Laurilliard b: Aug. 3/1803 No futher info.
L9) John George Laurilliard b: Feb. 2/1806
L 10) Maria Laurilliard b: ?
L 11) Christopher Laurilliard b: ?
L 12) ?
L 13) ?

L1) Thomas Laurilliard married Mary Ann Litchfield, a widow (1775-1826). Thomas died on Nov. 9/1830.

L2) Sarah Laurilliard married John Burness (Burns), who was born in Ireland. They migrated to Mass., USA. They had **children**:
L2.1) Matthew Burns b: 1833 Boston
Married Betsey E. Aldrich in 1859. They had no children. Matthew worked in a cotton mill in Shirley, Mass., later becoming a Flagman for a railroad.
L2.2) George E. Burns b: 1835 d: Nov. 15/1862
Married Rosella C. Lassell (b: 1840). They had **children**: Ella, Lucius, George E.
L2.3) Joseph Ward Burness b: Sept. 16/1838, d: Jan. 13/1911
Married Ella A. Plante. They had **children**: Joseph C., Charles W. & more.

L3) Henry Laurilliard was a Sailmaker in Halifax. He married Sarah Godfrey, a widow (her maiden name was probably Freeman). She was b: 1791 in Liverpool, d: 1870. They had **children**:
L3.1) Sarah Ann Freeman Laurilliard b: Oct. 14/1810 No further information.
L3.2) Henry George Lothrop Laurilliard b: Nov. 29/1812
L3.3) William Laurilliard b: June 25/1815

L3.4) Albert Laurilliard [LRef102] b: Oct. 19/1818
L3.5) Edwin Laurilliard b: Jan. 21/1821 No further information.

L3.2) Henry Laurilliard was a Master or Merchant Tailor [LRef3.2] on Hollis Street in Halifax. He was Secretary and Treasurer of the Halifax Temperance Hall Company in 1864-65. He married Matilda Rogers in 1835.

H. G. Laurilliard,
TAILOR,
GENTLEMEN'S DRESS MATERIALS
AND
Furnishing Goods, constantly on hand.
Agent for New York FASHION PLATES.
231 HOLLIS STREET,
HALIFAX, N. S.

Henry Salter Laurilliard

Children: M. Henrietta Laurilliard (b: 1845) who married Thomas E. Cooke in 1867; Fanny Laurilliard (b: 1849) who married George Alexander Barss, a farmer from Aylesford in 1873; Henry Salter Laurilliard (b: 1836, d: 1900) who was a tinsmith at Windsor, later becoming a mail carrier in Halifax. (He married twice, first to Sarah J. Winters in 1860, second, in 1875 to Mary Burke b: PEI; Charles DeW Laurilliard (b: 1841, d: at Country Harbour in 1909), who was a Tailor and soldier, and who married Sarah Mason, daughter of John and Lydia Mason of Country Harbour; Emma T. Laurilliard (b: 1849, who never married.

L3.3) See [LRef101] for more information.

L3.4) Albert Laurilliard was a Piano Maker. He married Mary Osborne on March 18/1840. They migrated to various parts of Canada and the USA, ending in San Jose, CA., where they settled. **Children**: Henry Laurilliard, who was a Music Master, and was in business with his father; Mary Laurillard, who married George R. Bent. Osborne Laurillard was a Piano Repairer and migrated to San Francisco, where he died in 1872. Arthur Laurillard lived in Oregon and was in the piano business. Annie Laurillard married John Gosbee, who also migrated to California. See (LRef102) for more information.

L4) William Laurillard was a Shipwright in Halifax. He married Elizabeth Caroline Scott in 1809. John Gosbee was one of the bondsmen for their Marriage Bond. **Children**:

L4.1) Eleanora Frances Laurillard b: Aug. 18/1811
L4.2) Mary Jane Laurillard b: Feb. 25/1814
L4.3) Martha S. Laurillard b: Apr. 13/1825
L4.4) Alexander McRae Laurillard b: Oct. 6/1820 d: 1908
L4.5) William John Scott Laurillard b: Nov. 21/1815

L4.4) Alexander Laurillard migrated to Philadelphia, PA. He married Ellen _____ and had at least one **child**, Mary Ellen Laurillard, who was born and died in 1864.

L4.5) See (LRef101) for more information.

L6) George Laurilliard was a shoemaker in Halifax. He married Mary Ann Heckman (b: Lunenburg 1808, d: 1873) in 1832. He is buried in Harrietsfield. They had **children**: Anne Laurilliard (b: @1841), who married John O'Donnell, a tailor who was born in Ireland (a daughter or granddaughter of the O'Donnells was one of the earliest female doctors graduated from Dalhousie University/Medical School); George Laurilliard (b: @1844), who married Katherine (Kate) Hayes and migrated to the USA, where they had a large family; Cecilia Isabella Laurilliard (b: @1852), who married John Crowell, a mason, in 1869; Lucy Laurilliard (b: @1842), who married George Fraser, a widower farmer at Harrietsfield; Thomas James Laurilliard, (b: @1849), who was a shoecutter, not married, and died of TB in May, 1871 in Mass., USA; Sarah Jane Laurilliard, (b: @1854).

L9) John George Laurilliard (b: Feb. 2/1806, d: @1896), was a Shipwright in Halifax. He married Susan Ann Smith (b: Chester @1805, d: @1897) on May 24/1840. They had 3 **children** in 1861, one male and 2 females but I can only find record of Agnes A. Laurilliard (b: @1849, d: 1910), a dressmaker, who never married.

L 10) Maria Laurilliard married George South, Jr., a Tailor in Halifax. They had **children**: John George South (b: Sept. 12/1814), Maria South (b: May 11/1820), Charles South (b Apr. 2/1823), Thomas South (b: Apr. 4/1825), Sarah Jane South (b: Oct. 17/1827), Henry Christopher South (b: Mar. 10/1830), Joseph Kefler South (b: July 10/1833).

L 11) Christopher Laurilliard was a carpenter. He married Grace _____. They had a **son**: Edward Laurilliard (b @1835, d: Newport, Hants Co.), married twice: 2nd to Sarah Margaret Brown in 1872 and had a son Arthur Edward Laurilliard (b: 1877). *Arthur's son, Frank, was killed in the Halifax Explosion.*

REFERENCES – LAURILLIARD

(LRef001) ***Nova Scotia's Montbéliard Names***, by Terrence M. Punch

(LRef100) Fleet Marriages -

Before Lord Hardwicke's Marriage Act of 1754, marriages did not legally have to take place in church. In the late 17th century about a half of all marriages in London were clandestine marriages with no questions asked, with no banns or licences. One of the most well known centre for clandestine marriages was the Fleet Prison. Fleet marriages took place in the area just around the Fleet prison by clergymen debtors, and all types of people were married here.

(LRef101) William Lorillard was either a son of L3.2) Henry Laurilliard OR a son of L4) William Laurilliard. They both had a son named William in the year 1815. All of the records I checked had differing dates for his birth; none exactly matched anything else.

William Laurilliard migrated to Bexar Co., Texas and lived in the San Antonio area. He married a widow with children, Hannah

Maria (Wright) Weatherspoon Huntress. He was a soldier in the US Civil War, Company K, 6th Texas Infantry (and also the Second Dragoons). He died at Tennessee*, "...due to disease, probably dysentery", in July/1863. *A newspaper report gives place of death as Dalton, GA, in 1864.

Children: Alexander Lorillard, William Lorillard (b: June 13, 1852, d: July, 1935); Thomas Lorillard (b: 1857); Eleanor Lorillard (b: 1858, d: 1945); James Lorillard (b: 1861). There is more information available on this branch of the family in Texas and other western states' records.

(LRef102) From ***The History of Santa Clara County***:

Albert Laurilliard was born in Halifax in 1817, where he remained until nineteen years of age, receiving his education in the national schools, during which time he commenced to learn the piano-making business. In 1836 he came to the United States and settled in Boston, where he continued at his trade and then removed to New York, where he learned more of the business. He spent a number of years in Boston, New York, and in Halifax, NS. While living in Halifax. he did most of the repairing of pianos in that section of the British Provinces. In 1868 he removed to Chicago, Illinois, and engaged in the same business, his special interests requiring him to travel throughout the Western States. In 1872 he came to San Jose and established himself in his present business, which he has since conducted.

Mr. Laurilliard was married, in 1838 to Miss Mary Osborne, a native of Scotland. Five **children** were born to this marriage: Henry, in business with his father; Mary, the wife of George R. Bent, of San Jose; Osborne, who died in San Francisco in 1872; Arthur, in the piano business in Oregon; and Annie, the widow of the late **John G. Gosbee**, of San Jose. Mr. Laurilliard descends from a French Huguenot family, who removed to England from France during the Huguenot troubles, and afterward to America, and located in Nova Scotia, where his branch of the family received a grant of land from the British Government. Mr. Laurilliard's whole life has been devoted to music, and to the improvement and development of musical instruments.

*There is a **Laurilliard** piano in the New Brunswick Museum, St. John*

– The Canadian Encyclopedia of Music.

(LRef3.2) From: ***Fashion, A Canadian Perspective,*** Page 168, by Alexandra Palmer:

"In 1858 there were nineteen tailors listed in the city (Halifax) directory. Ten years later there were only eight tailors listed, but twenty-one merchant tailors, some of whom were registered as clothiers as well. Some drygood merchants, who were traditional wholesalers of non-perishable groceries, hardware, and imported British fabrics, also began manufacturing men's and boy's garments at this time. Advertisements in the city directories stressed the particular strength of the business. ... The style conscious Mr. H. G. Laurilliard of 231 Hollis street was an 'Agent for New York Fashion plates.'

Found online at: **Treasurenet.com**, posted by romeo-1, who gave me permission to use this photo.

Additional Notes

There were a few Laurillairds with the name of George, and I cannot place one of them. The 1861 Census lists 5 Laurilliards: Albert in Kings County, H.G, John and George in Halifax County, and George in Hants County.

A George Laurilliard married Isabella Trider in 1845. This George was the father of Lewis, Grace, Jane, and Laura Mary. Lewis was a blacksmith. He married Alice F. Wilson in Windsor, and raised a large familfy in Falmouth, Hants County.

There are other Laurilliards I cannot place:

- Alphonso G. F. Laurilliard, born @1849 in Nova Scotia, who married and lived in Georgetown, Mass.
- Richard Laurilliard, who was a Bookbinder in Halifax in 1866-1867 and is listed in Hutchinson's Directory. He never married and died, age 70, at the Halifax City Home in 1915.
- Edward Laurilliard, a tailor, who shows up on the 1850 US Census in Industry, Maine. He married Arvilla W. Sanders.

INDEX

www.ingramcontent.com/pod-product-compliance
Ingram Content Group UK Ltd.
Pitfield, Milton Keynes, MK11 3LW, UK
UKHW020238250726
13967UKWH00001B/430

9 780557 731473